craft
tree

Patchwork Pillows

compiled by **Lindsey Murray McClelland**

INTERWEAVE.
interweave.com

Interweave grants permission to
photocopy the templates in this
publication for personal use.

*The projects in this collection were
originally published in other Interweave
publications, including* 101 Patchwork,
Modern Patchwork, Quilt Scene,
Quilting Arts, *and* Stitch *magazines
and 'QATV.' Some have been altered to
update information and/or conform to
space limitations.*

Interweave Press LLC
A division of F+W Media, Inc
201 East Fourth Street
Loveland, CO 80537
interweave.com

Manufactured in the United States
by Versa Press

ISBN 978-1-59668-767-7 (pbk.)

Table of Contents

4 Living Room Pillows

5 **Quilted Patchwork Pillow Cover**
Amy Ellis

6 **The Great Quilted Pillow**
Erin Daniels

8 **Asymmetrical Log Cabin Pillow**
Lisa Congdon

10 **Log Cabin Patchwork Pillow for Grandpa**
Sherry Goshon

12 Whimsical Pillows

13 **Cupcake Pillow**
Donna Babylon

17 **Hanging Flags Fusible-Appliqué Pillow**
Melissa Lunden

19 Fly-Away Pillow
Melissa Frantz

22 Mod Pillow Pair
Melissa Lunden

24 Tufted Floor Pillow
Carol Zentgraf

26 Tuesday Pillow
Malka Dubrawsky

30 Pi Pillow
Malka Dubrawsky

33 Decorative Bed Pillows

34 Serenity Sham
Donna Babylon

35 Reverse Appliqué Pillow
Kevin Kosbab

37 Cute-as-a-Button Pillow
Tricia Waddell

39 Modern Eyelet Pillow
Blair Stocker

41 Bejeweled Pillow
Blair Stocker

43 Mixed-Media Pillow Cover
Julie Fei-Fan Balzer

45 Weeds & Wildflowers Sofa Pillow
Margaret Applin

46 Circles, Stitches & Dye
Jill Brummett Tucker

49 Holiday Ornament Pillow
Debbie Grifka

51 Sewing Basics

LIVING ROOM PILLOWS

Materials

—Variety of scraps or fat quarters for the pieced front

—Fabric for backing the pillow front, 20" × 20" (51 × 51 cm) square

—Batting, 20" × 20" (51 × 51 cm) square

—Fabric for the envelope backing, ½ yd (45.5 cm)

—Pillow form, 18" × 18" (45.5 × 45.5 cm)

—Rotary cutting supplies

Finished Size

18" × 18" (45.5 × 45.5 cm)

note

✳ Use ¼" (6 mm) seam allowances throughout.

Directions

1 From a variety of fabrics, cut 10 squares 2" × 2" (5 × 5 cm). These will be the centers of your pieced blocks. Also cut 9 squares 3½" × 3½" (9 × 9 cm). These will be the plain squares in the pillow top; set them aside until Step 5.

2 Select a variety of fabrics to surround the 2" (5 cm) block center squares, and cut 10 strips 1¼" × 12" (3.2 × 30.5 cm). From each strip, cut 2 rectangles 1¼" × 2" (3.2 × 5 cm) and 2 rectangles 1¼" × 3½" (3.2 × 9 cm). Using matching strips, sew the 1¼" × 2" (3.2 × 5 cm) strips to opposite sides of the 2" (5 cm)squares, and then sew the 1¼" × 3½" (3.2 × 9 cm) rectangles to the top and bottom. Press the seam allowances away from the block center as you work.

3 Select 4 of the small pieced blocks to build upon. (Set aside the remaining 6 small pieced blocks.) Select fabrics for the next round, and cut 4 strips 2" × 21" (5 × 53.5 cm). From each strip, cut 2 rectangles 2" × 3½"

Tip

I found it helpful to arrange the design in quadrants, allocating the 9½" (24 cm) block to 1 quadrant, (1) 6½" (16.5 cm) block to each of the remaining quadrants, and moving the 3½" (9 cm) squares around to fill in and add variety.

Quilted Patchwork Pillow Cover

by Amy Ellis

I made this pillow cover for a swap I participated in online. Inspired by my partner's favorite quilts and pillows, I pulled many fabrics that were small in scale, and I started building a palette. The variety of block sizes makes for fun options with the overall design. This pillow cover can easily be made in a leisurely afternoon, and it suits any home décor. Start with one inspirational piece of fabric and pull in others that work with it. Don't forget to add some contrast. Enjoy the process!

(5 × 9 cm) and 2 rectangles 2" × 6½" (5 × 16.5 cm). Then sew them to the pieced center squares in the same manner as in Step 2.

4 Select 1 of these larger pieced blocks and add 1 more round to it. Cut a 2" × 33" (5 × 84 cm) strip, and from it cut 2 rectangles 2" × 6½" (5 × 16.5 cm) and 2 rectangles 2" × 9½" (5 × 24 cm). Sew these to your block.

Tip

Piece 1 quadrant at a time. Sew (2) 3½" (9 cm) squares together and join them to the side of (1) 6½" (16.5 cm) square. Sew the remaining 3½" (9 cm) squares together in a row and sew to the pieced unit to complete the quadrant. Piece the remaining quadrants, and then sew them together.

5 Lay out your blocks in a pleasing arrangement.

6 Sew the squares together to complete the pillow front.

7 Baste the pillow front together with the 20" (51 cm) squares of batting and backing fabric; quilt. I used diagonal lines, intentionally omitting some lines to add interest.

8 Trim away the excess batting and backing fabric.

9 From the fabric for the envelope backing, cut 2 rectangles 11" × 18½" (28 × 47 cm). Add a rolled hem to (1) 18½" (47 cm) side of both rectangles.

10 With the pillow front facing up, place the 2 rectangles on top, right sides down and hemmed edges overlapping in the middle. Match the raw edges and the corners of the front and back pieces, and pin the layers together. The back rectangles will overlap about 2" (5 cm) in the center.

11 Sew around the edges. Finish the seam by sewing around a second time with a zigzag stitch to prevent fraying.

12 Turn the cover right-side out and press flat. Add your pillow form and enjoy! 🍃

Visit **AMY ELLIS'S** website at amyscreativeside.com.

The Great Quilted Pillow
by Erin Daniels

Quilted pillows provide all the elements of a full-size quilt in a fun and manageable scale that encourages a sense of immediate accomplishment and excitement. They are a great low-stakes environment for designing your own simple patterns and experimenting with color/fabric combinations. So, if you want to build up your quilting skills, or if you are just looking for a fun, small home-dec project, try your hand at these quilted pillows!

Materials

- (45) 1¾" × 7" (4.5 × 18 cm) strips of patterned fabric (use 5 different fabrics; cut 9 strips from each fabric) for the blocks

- 4½" (11.5 cm) square quilting ruler (or a 4½" [11.5 cm] square template)

- (6) 1¾" × 4½" (4.5 × 11.5 cm) strips of white fabric for the vertical sashing between blocks

- (2) 1¾" × 15" (4.5 × 38 cm) strips of white fabric for the horizontal sashing between rows

- (2) 2" × 15" (5 × 38 cm) strips of white fabric for the left and right sashing

- (2) 2" × 18" (5 × 45.5 cm) strips of white fabric for the top and bottom sashing

- (1) 20" × 20" (51 × 51 cm) piece of lightweight batting

- (1) 20" × 20" (51 × 51 cm) piece of fabric to back the pillow front (This fabric will not be visible in the finished pillows.)

- (2) 12½" × 18" (31.5 × 45.5 cm) pieces of fabric for the envelope backing of the pillow

- Binding fabric, 2½" × 90" (6.5 × 228.5 cm)

- 18" (45.5 cm) square pillow form

Directions

1 Referring to the materials list, cut the fabrics for this project.

2 Group the 45 strips of patterned fabrics into 9 sets of 5 strips each (each set should have 1 of each of the 5 different fabrics). Sew each set of strips together along the long side using a ¼" (6 mm) seam allowance (vary the order of the strips for each block). Press the seams.

3 Place the 4½" (11.5 cm) square quilting ruler or template on-point in the center of the first pieced strip set, so that each corner of the template is centered along each side of the pieced strip set. Trim to size (4½" [11.5 cm] square). Cut all 9 blocks in this manner.

4 Arrange the blocks in a pleasing order and sew each row of 3 blocks together with a 1¾" × 4½" (4.5 × 11.5 cm) white sashing strip between each block. Press the seams.

5 Sew the 3 rows together, with a 1¾" × 15" (4.5 × 38 cm) sashing strip between each row. Press the seams.

6 Sew the 15" (38 cm) sashing strips to the left and right edges of the pillow top. Press. Then sew the 18" (45.5 cm) sashing strips to the top and bottom. Press. At this point, the pillow top should measure 18" × 18" (45.5 × 45.5 cm).

7 Make a quilt sandwich with the pillow top, batting, and pillow top backing. Baste together.

Note: This backing fabric will not be visible in the completed pillow.

8 Quilt around each block, just barely inside and outside of the seam. Then quilt the sashing between the blocks with straight lines slightly less than ⅜" (1 cm) apart.

9 Quilt around the outer-edge sashing with lines slightly less than ⅜" (1 cm) apart. Trim the excess batting and backing; square the corners while trimming.

10 With the (2) 12½" × 18" (31.5 × 45.5 cm) pieces of fabric for the envelope backing of the pillow, create a hem along (1) 18" (45.5 cm) side of each piece by folding the edge in ⅜" (1 cm) twice toward the wrong side; press and then stitch in place.

11 Position the quilted pillow top wrong-side up on your work surface. Line up one of the backing pieces (right side facing up) on top of the pillow top back, with the finished edge toward the center. Repeat with the other backing piece on the other side, so that the 2 backing pieces are overlapping, creating an envelope, with the finished edges toward the center. Stitch around the edges using a scant ¼" (6 mm) seam.

12 Attach the binding using your favorite binding method. Place the pillow form inside the cover and admire! 🖊

Visit **ERIN DANIELS'S** website at whittlestitch.blogspot.com.

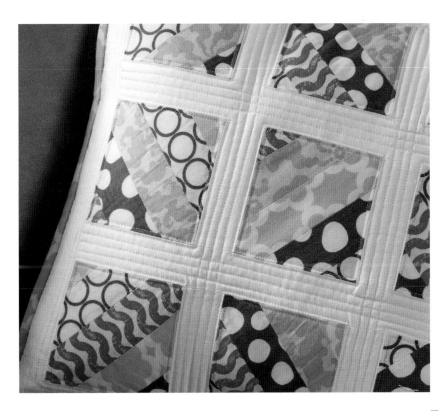

Materials

—⅛ yd (11.5 cm) each of 6–10 different cotton fabrics with a mixture of solids and prints

—⅝ yd (57 cm) of solid cotton fabric for pillow back

—Matching sewing thread

—21" × 21" (53.5 × 53.5 cm) square of cotton batting

—38" (96.5 cm) of 1¼" (3.2 cm) wide ribbon

—18" (45.5 cm) square pillow form

—Rotary cutter and self-healing mat

—Acrylic quilt ruler

Finished Size

18 × 18" (45.5 × 45.5 cm)

----

note

✽ All seam allowances are ¼" (6 mm) unless otherwise indicated.

Directions

Cut out and mark fabric

1 Using a rotary cutter and quilt ruler, cut patches for the log cabin center to the following sizes: 1¾" × 2⅛" (4.5 × 5.5 cm), 1¾" × 1⅞" (4.5 × 5 cm), and 2¼" × 3½" (5.5 × 9 cm).

2 Cut 5–8 strips of various lengths (about 6"–15" [15–38 cm]) and widths of each fabric for pillow top. My strips ranged from 1¾"–2¼" (4.5–5.5 cm) wide. Don't worry too much about the length of the strips; they just need to be progressively longer than the 4" (10 cm) piece you'll be sewing to (each time you add a strip you'll press and then trim the strip ends even with the patchwork). Longer strips will give you more freedom to place them as you wish, as the pillow top is built from longer and longer strips as you piece your way toward the outer edges of the pillow.

Piecing the pillow top

3 Stitch the 1¾" × 2⅛" (4.5 × 5.5 cm) and 1¾" × 1⅞" (4.5 × 5 cm) patches together along the 1¾" (4.5 cm) edge. Press the seam. Add the 2¼" × 3½" (5.5 × 9 cm) rectangle to complete the center square; press.

4 Begin building outward in the pattern shown in **figure 1**, by beginning to stitch the fabric strips to the center square. You can either

Asymmetrical Log Cabin Pillow

by Lisa Congdon

This modern take on traditional log cabin quilts places the center square off center and pieces strips of different widths and fabrics to build the pillow top. The free-form design and contemporary color, give this pillow a truly inspired feel.

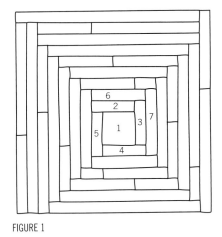

FIGURE 1

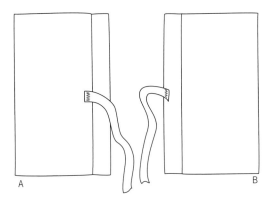

A   B

FIGURE 2

follow the pattern I used or make up your own as you go along. I like to place my center square "off center" to create a pillow that is not perfectly symmetrical.

5 Press after each strip addition, pressing the seam toward the center square. Then trim the strip ends even with the existing patchwork and square up as needed. Repeat this process for each strip.

6 Continue building in this way, paying attention to balance of overall color and pattern. As the pillow square becomes larger, try piecing strips from two or three different fabrics for variation and interest. Vary the width of the strips as you build the pillow square in different directions. This gives your pillow square a less traditional, more modern feel.

7 When your pillow square measures at least 19" × 19" (48.5 × 48.5 cm), stop adding strips. If your patchwork is slightly larger, that's okay; it will be trimmed after quilting.

Sew pillow top to batting

8 Center your pillow square on the cotton batting and pin it down in eight to twelve different spots from the center to the outer edge. You will remove the pins as you begin the machine quilting, so placement is not as important as much as ensuring that the pillow square is secured to the batting before you begin quilting. The batting is cut slightly oversized; this ensures that you will have ample batting out to the edge of your pillow square in the event that the batting bunches slightly while quilting.

9 Begin machine-quilting by stitching concentric squares around the pillow, following the lines of the strips. Stitch in one long line by turning corners, rather than creating closed squares. You can stitch the lines as closely as you want and vary the widths between lines of stitching for added interest. Always begin your quilting from the center square of your pillow—even if your center square is not in the center!

10 Once your piece is quilted, trim it to 19" × 19" (48.5 × 48.5 cm).

Make the pillow backing

11 To make the pillow backing, cut two 19" × 13" (48.5 × 33 cm) rectangles of the fabric that you have set aside for the back. Hem one 19" (48.5 cm) edge as follows: fold over 2" (5 cm) to the wrong side; press and zigzag stitch along the raw edge. Repeat with the second piece. These are pieces A and B.

12 Turn the 2 back pieces over so the turned edges are facing down. Sew a 19" (48.5 cm) length of ribbon at the center of piece A (**figure 2**, left side), using a zigzag stitch (tuck the raw edge of the ribbon under about ¼" [6 mm]), and placing the ribbon directly over the zigzag stitching on the right top side of the fabric (**figure 2**, left side). Reinforce the stitching a few times.

13 Repeat Step 12 to attach the second piece of the ribbon to piece B (**figure 2**, right side), at the center, but this time placing it close to the folded edge (**figure 2**, right side).

Assembly

14 To finish the pillow, lay the quilted patchwork top right-side up. Take back piece A and lay it on top of the patchwork, right sides facing, so that the folded edge with the ribbon is laying in the middle of the patchwork top. Match up the bottom corners and pin.

15 Lay down back piece B the same way, but with the top corners matching. The 2 back pieces should overlap in the middle by about 2" (5 cm). Pin in place.

16 Machine stitch around all four sides, using a ½" (1.3 cm) seam allowance. Remove the pins and turn the pillow cover right-side out. Slide in your pillow form and tie the ribbons to close the pillow back. 🖋

LISA CONGDON'S projects have been published in *Adorn* and *Readymade* magazines and she is featured in *The Crafter's Companion* (Snowbooks, 2006). Visit her website at lisacongdon.com.

Materials

—Finished size varies depending on photo size and strip widths (featured pillow is 13½" × 19" [34.5 × 48.5 cm])

—1 sheet 8½" × 11" (21.5 × 28 cm) ink-jet fabric sheets, such as EQ Printables (See "Making Fabric Sheets for your Ink-jet Printer" if you wish to make your own.)

—Favorite photo (as a digital file on your computer, or a printout)

—Ink-jet printer

—4–5 assorted fabrics for the log-cabin strips, ⅛–¼ yd (11.5–23 cm) each (I incorporated the backing fabric as one of my strip fabrics.)

—Embroidery thread and needle

—1 fat quarter of fabric for the back (I used Ultrasuede.)

—Stuffing

---

note

* The finished pillow size will vary depending on the size of your photo. Feel free to vary the strip sizes, depending on what will be most appealing for your design.

Directions

Print the photo on fabric

1 Load the printable fabric paper into your printer. You can use the printer as a copier and copy your favorite photo, or scan it into your computer and just print.

2 If you wish to add any design elements to your image, do so now. I typed the word "Grandpa" underneath the photo.

3 Print the photo onto the fabric, following the manufacturer's instructions.

Construct the pillow

4 Determine the amount of white area you wish to have around the outside of your photo, and then allow for ¼" (6 mm) seam allowances before you trim the photo to size. If you wish to add a line of running stitches below the image like I did, be sure to allow for this area inside the seam allowance. Trim the excess fabric from around the photo. After trimming my

Log Cabin Patchwork Pillow FOR GRANDPA

by Sherry Goshon

Sewn gifts for men aren't the easiest thing to come up with. But this pillow features a photo of my husband's hand with one of our granddaughter's hands, and he fell in love with it. I used cotton fabrics that match our living room and backed the pillow with Ultrasuede. The patchwork is a basic log cabin pattern, but with a twist since the strips aren't the same each time.

photo it measured 5¾" × 8½" (14.5 × 21.5 cm).

Note: Steps 2–6 will lead you to cut and add strips that match my design. Feel free to adjust the strip widths and fabric order as desired for your pillow design. You can see in the process photos I used a different photo, so that pillow will be an entirely different size than the featured Grandpa pillow.

5 Cut a 1⅞" (5 cm) wide strip to be stitched to the top of the photo. (I used the backing fabric for this piece.) Sew this strip to the top of your photo fabric (**figure 1**). Press open, and then cut off the excess length.

6 Select the fabric to be sewn to the left and right sides of the photo. Cut a 3" (7.5 cm) wide strip, and sew it to 1 side of the photo. Press open and trim even. Using the remaining strip length, repeat the process on the other side of the photo (**figure 2**).

7 Select the fabric to be sewn to the top and bottom. Cut a 4" (10 cm) wide strip, and sew it to the top. Press open and trim even. Repeat for the bottom.

8 Select the fabric for the left edge. Cut a 4¾" (12 cm) wide strip, and sew it to the left side. Press open and trim even.

9 Select the fabric for the right edge. Cut a 3" (7.5 cm) wide strip, and sew it to the right side. Press open and trim even.

10 Using embroidery thread, sew a running stitch along 1 edge of the photo fabric, if you wish (**figure 3**).

11 Press the patchwork pillow front.

12 Cut the backing fabric the same size as the pillow front.

13 Layer the pillow front on the backing, right sides together. Stitch all the way around the pillow, leaving a 4" (10 cm) opening at the bottom.

14 Turn the pillow right-side out, stuff it firmly, and then stitch the opening closed. 🖉

Visit **SHERRY GOSHON'S** website at sherrygoshonart.com.

FIGURE 1

FIGURE 2

FIGURE 3

Process photos by Sherry Goshon

Making Fabric Sheets for Your Ink-jet Printer

Materials

—Cotton fabric: white or off-white

—Freezer paper

—Bubble Jet Set 2000 and Jet Rinse Set

1. Following the manufacturer's instructions, prepare the white fabric with the Bubble Jet Set 2000. Let the fabric dry.

2. Cut a piece of freezer paper 8½" × 11" (21.5 × 28 cm).

3. Iron the freezer paper to the fabric and cut the fabric to match. Iron; then flip the fabric over and iron again on the back side. I do this several times to make sure there are no bubbles or wrinkles.

4. Load the fabric paper into your printer. You can use the printer as a copier and copy your favorite photo, or scan it into your computer and just print.

5. Once the image has printed, follow the manufacturer's instructions to use the Jet Rinse Set.

Let dry.

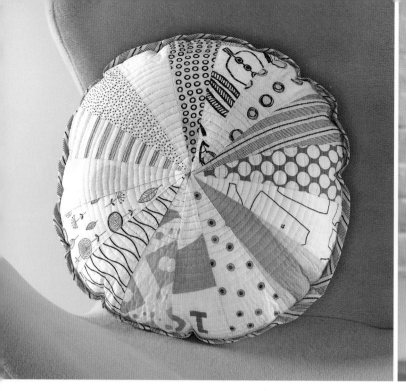

WHIMSICAL PILLOWS

Cupcake Pillow
by Donna Babylon

Enjoy a calorie-free cupcake with this whimsical pillow that cheers up any room. The body of the pillow is made with fleece, then embellished with double-edge ruffle "icing" made from gathered cotton strips and a pom-pom cherry.

Materials

—½ yd (45.5 cm) each of 2 colors of 60" (152.5 cm) wide fleece for pillow Bottom, Back, and Top (*shown:* blue and white)

—½ yd (45.5 cm) of 45" (114.5 cm) wide print cotton fabric for ruffle icing (*shown:* pink "sprinkles" print)

—Tear-away stabilizer (optional, if using satin stitch)

—Matching sewing thread for all 3 fabrics used

—1½" (3.8 cm) diameter red pom-pom for cherry

—Fiberfill (one bag)

—Rotary cutter, self-healing mat, and rigid gridded acrylic ruler (optional)

—Water-soluble fabric marker

—Point turner

—Handsewing needle

—Cupcake templates on pages 15–16

Finished Size
16" wide × 15" tall × 3" deep
(40.5 × 38 × 7.5 cm)

notes

* All seam allowances are ½" (1.3 cm) unless otherwise indicated.

* For explanations of terms and techniques and/or help with pattern markings, see Sewing Basics.

* Fleece has a nap (directional texture), so make sure all pattern pieces are placed on the fabric in the same direction.

Directions
Cut fabric

1 Using the provided pattern pieces, cut one Back and one Bottom from the blue fleece, and one Top from the white fleece (or using your chosen colors). Transfer the vertical guidelines on the Bottom piece to the right side of the fabric with a water-soluble fabric marker. *Optional:* If you plan to use a satin stitch to create the ridges in the bottom of the cupcake, cut one piece of tear-away stabilizer slightly larger than the Bottom.

2 From the cotton print for the ruffle icing, cut:
—1 piece 5" × 24" (12.5 × 61 cm)

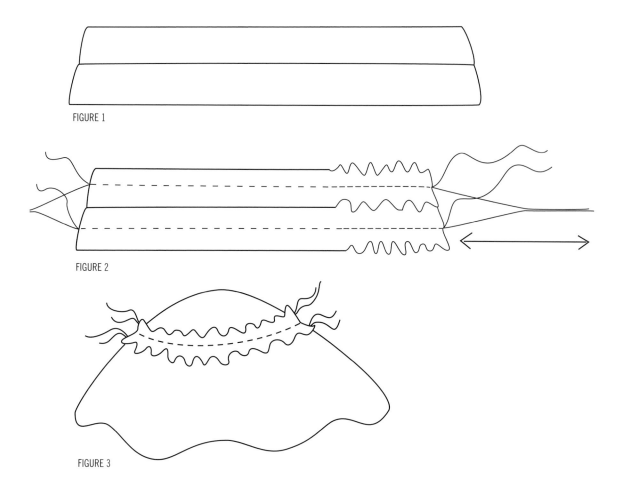

FIGURE 1

FIGURE 2

FIGURE 3

—1 piece 5" × 28" (12.5 × 71 cm)
—1 piece 5" × 31" (12.5 × 79 cm)

Embellish the bottom and prepare ruffle icing

3 Using thread to match the Bottom fabric, either straight stitch (2.5–3.0 mm long) or satin-stitch (1.5–2.0 mm wide and 0.3–0.4 mm long) directly on the transferred lines to create the illusion of the folds in the cupcake paper. If satin stitching, place the tear-away stabilizer under the fleece for stitch stability. Do not remove the stabilizer yet. *Note:* Experiment with stitch length and width settings on a scrap first, to make sure the chosen stitch will feed smoothly across the fleece.

4 Fold each cotton print strip in half lengthwise right sides together and stitch together along the long edge, leaving the short ends open. Press the seams open and turn the tubes right-side out.

5 Center the seam of each tube and press smooth and flat (this way, the seam won't show at all from one side of the flattened tube).

6 Cut each short tube end at a diagonal **(figure 1)**.

7 Adjust your machine for a gathering stitch. Place one icing tube, seam side down, under the needle and stitch ¾" (2 cm) from each long

pressed edge. Do not backtack at either end and be sure to leave long thread tails. Repeat the entire step with each of the remaining tubes.

8 Tightly grasp the bobbin threads only at one end of the first tube. With your free hand, gently slide the fabric over the threads, away from the ends being held and toward the center of the strip, to create the gathers **(figure 2)**. Adjust your grasp as needed on the bobbin threads as the tube becomes gathered. Stop sliding the fabric at the middle of the strip and repeat the process from the other end. Use the rows of gathering stitches to gather the shortest tube to about 11" (28 cm) long, the middle tube to about 14" (35.5 cm) long, and the longest tube to about 15½" (39.5 cm) long. *Note:* Be gentle as you create the gathers to avoid breaking the thread. If the thread breaks, release the gathers completely and resew the gathering stitches, then make a fresh start.

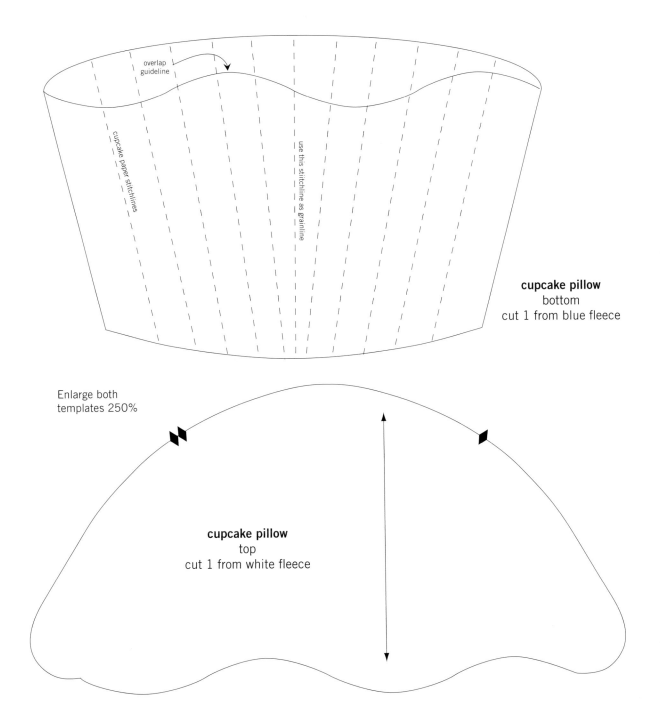

cupcake pillow
bottom
cut 1 from blue fleece

overlap guideline

cupcake paper stitchlines

use this stitchline as grainline

Enlarge both
templates 250%

cupcake pillow
top
cut 1 from white fleece

Arrange ruffle icing

9 Evenly distribute the gathers along each tube.

10 Refer to the photograph on page 13 to arrange the three rows of ruffles on the Top piece (or arrange them as desired). Adjust the ruffles to fit by either tightening or loosening the gathers. The diagonal edges of the ruffles should roughly match the contoured shape of the Top piece. Pin the ruffles in place.

11 Change thread to match the ruffle icing and, using a regular stitch length, topstitch each ruffle directly down the center, between the basting stitches **(figure 3)**. When all 3 ruffles have been attached, remove all basting stitches.

Attach top to bottom

12 Using the guidelines on the pattern, place the Top piece over the Bottom piece, with right sides facing up. Pin in place.

13 Stitch the Top to the Bottom following the curved lower edge of the Top with either a medium-wide satin stitch (3.0 mm wide and 0.3–0.4 mm long) or a straight stitch and thread that matches the cupcake Top. Carefully remove the stabilizer if still in place.

14 On the wrong side of the attached pieces, trim away the excess Bottom fabric to within ⅛" (3 mm) of the stitching line.

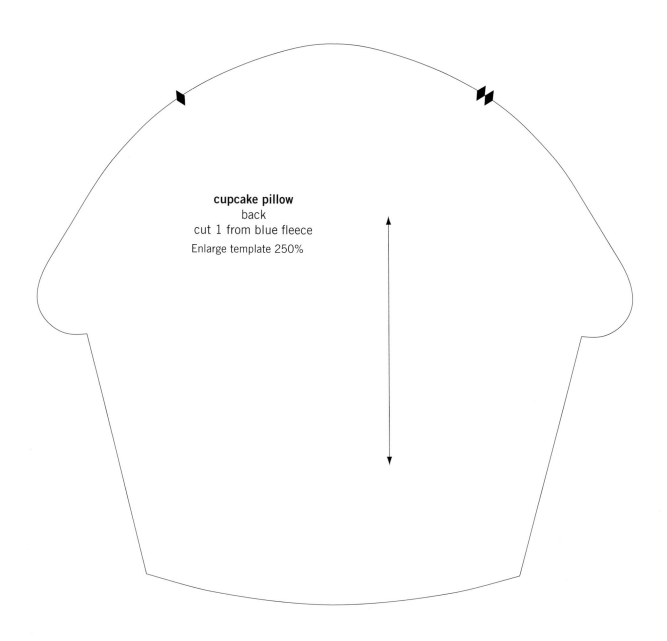

cupcake pillow
back
cut 1 from blue fleece
Enlarge template 250%

Finish pillow

15 Pin the Back piece to the assembled cupcake front, right sides together. Be sure to push the icing gathers out of the way so they will not be trapped in the seam but do catch the icing raw edges in the seam. Stitch around the entire shape of the pillow, leaving a 5" (12.5 cm) opening along the bottom edge for turning and stuffing.

16 Clip any curved seam allowances, every ½" (1.3 cm). To avoid bulk, trim the seam allowance diagonally at the corners.

17 Turn the pillow right-side out and insert the point turner into the opening. Use the tool to push out the corners and smooth the rounded areas.

18 Handsew the pom-pom "cherry" to the top of the cupcake.

19 Using the fiberfill, stuff the pillow to the desired fullness. To stuff, take a handful of fiberfill and fluff the fibers with your fingers to remove any clumps. Begin filling the corners and small sections of the pillow, working toward the center of the pillow to stuff the remaining areas.

20 Handstitch the opening closed with a slip stitch. 🖋

DONNA BABYLON is the author of *Decorating Sewlutions*. Visit her online at moresplashthancash.com.

Materials
—Pillow insert, 12" × 16" (30.5 × 40.5 cm)

—Fabric for the pillow cover (front and back), ½ yd (45.5 cm; I used Kona cotton in snow.)

—6 assorted prints for the flags (on pillow front and back), 4" × 6" (10 × 15 cm) rectangle each

—Fabric for the bird (front), 5" × 6" (12.5 × 15 cm) rectangle (I used Kona cotton in charcoal.)

—Fusible web, ½ yd (45.5 cm)

—Thread, off-white and dark gray

—Flag and Bird templates on page 18

—Fabric marking pen

Optional
—Invisible zipper, 16" (40.5 cm) or longer

—Yarn or heavy cord to use as a guide for marking the stitching line along the top of the flags, 20" (51 cm)

—Disappearing-ink fabric marker

Finished Size
12" × 16" (30.5 × 40.5 cm)

---

note

∗ The flag design is duplicated on the back of the pillow. The bird is featured on the pillow front only.

Directions

1 Apply fusible web to the 6 prints and to the fabric for the bird, following the manufacturer's directions.

2 Cut 2 triangles from each print, using the flag template.

3 Trace and cut out the bird, using the bird template.

4 Cut 2 rectangles 13" × 17" (33 × 43 cm) from the fabric for the pillow cover front and back.

5 Arrange the flags in a curve on the pillow front and back (remember to account for seam allowances along all outside edges); fuse. Position the bird on the pillow front (you'll be trimming the corners in the next step, so keep seam allowances and the trimming step in mind when you place the bird); fuse (figure 1).

6 To shape the pillow cover so it will better fit the pillow insert, mark the center of each side of the pillow

Hanging Flags Fusible-Appliqué Pillow
by Melissa Lunden

This pillow was inspired by one of the fabrics in the "Circa 52" fabric collection by Birch Fabrics. The theme translated well into a modern, whimsical quickly fused appliqué design. The instructions include a shaping technique to make the pillow cover fit the insert more snugly.

Tip

You may want to use a piece of yarn to help determine the curve of the stitching line. Use a disappearing ink fabric marker to trace along the yarn line, if you wish. (Be sure to test the disappearing-ink marker on your fabric before using it on your pillow.)

FIGURE 1

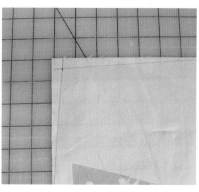

FIGURE 2

front and back pieces. Measure and mark ½" (1.3 cm) from each corner. Using a ruler, draw a line from the center mark to the corner mark **(figure 2)**.

7 Trim the pillow front and back following the marked lines **(figure 3)**.

8 With off-white thread, sew along the 2 bottom sides of the flags to secure them to the pillow. You can use a straight stitch, which will allow for a little fraying on the edges and give the pillow a slightly deconstructed look, or you can use a tight zigzag stitch.

9 Using dark gray thread, sew across the tops of the flags, from 1 side of the pillow to the other side. For a distinct look, use a tight zigzag stitch. Repeat this process on the pillow back fabric.

10 With the dark gray thread, sew along the edge of the bird to secure it to the pillow. I used a straight stitch along the edge of the bird in the featured finished pillow, but for the bird in the process photo I used a zigzag stitch.

Note: For the pillow closure, you can either insert an invisible zipper on the bottom of the pillow, or you can handsew the pillow closed after you have sewn the 3 sides of the pillow. If you opt for the invisible zipper, add it at this stage.

11 With the pillow front and back right sides together, sew the remaining 3 sides with a ½" (1.3 cm) seam allowance. Turn the pillow right-side out and press.

12 Place the pillow insert inside the pillow cover. Handstitch the seam closed if you chose to omit the zipper step. 🍃

Visit **MELISSA LUNDEN'S** website at lundendesigns.com.

FIGURE 3

Flag template

Bird template

Templates are actual size

Materials

—½ yd (45.5 cm) of brushed cotton canvas or medium-weight home decor cotton for front panel

—½ yd (45.5 cm) of coordinating print cotton for back panels

—2½ yd (2.3 m) of 1¾" (4.5 cm) wide single-fold bias tape or 1 fat quarter (18" × 20" [45.5 × 51 cm]) of coordinating cotton to make bias tape (*shown:* 2 different cotton print fabrics to create a varied length of bias tape)

—14" × 28" (35.5 × 71 cm) pillow form

—2½ yd (2.3 m) of ¼" (6 mm) wide upholstery piping cord

—Coordinating sewing thread

—Contrasting embroidery thread

—Handsewing needle

—Balloon templates (page 20)

—Fabric Paint (I used Jaquard Textile Color)

—Paintbrush (medium size)

—Freezer paper

—X-acto knife or paper blade

—Water-soluble fabric marker

—Zipper foot

Optional
—Rotary cutter and self-healing mat

—French curve

—Pinking shears or serger

Finished Size
14½ × 28½" (37 × 72.5 cm)

----
note

✳ All seam allowances are ½" (1.3 cm) unless otherwise noted.

Directions
Cut fabric

1 Cut a rectangle for the front panel from the cotton canvas or home decor cotton measuring 15" × 29" (38 × 73.5 cm).

2 With the front panel lying flat on a table in front of you, measure 2" (5 cm) over from one corner along the edge and mark, then measure 2" (5 cm) down the other edge from the same corner and mark. Repeat to mark the edges at the other three corners. Using a drinking glass or French

Fly-Away Pillow
by Melissa Frantz

Stenciled fabric paint and handstitching make happy red balloons on this comfy cotton-canvas pillow. Use a print for the envelope back and design your own corded piping as the final touch.

curve as a guide, draw a curve at each corner from mark to mark to create evenly rounded edges. Cut along the curved marks.

3 Cut two rectangles for the back panels from the coordinating cotton, each measuring 15" × 20" (38 × 51 cm).

Stencil balloons

4 Trace the balloon bunch template onto freezer paper, drawing on the matte (non-waxy) side. Using an X-acto knife and a cutting mat or scissors, carefully cut out each balloon, being careful not to cut into the paper connecting the balloons. On a separate piece of freezer paper, trace and cut the single balloon shape.

5 With the front panel facing right-side up, place the larger stencil (waxy side down) on the front panel, positioning it about 5" (12.5 cm) from the left (short) side of the pillow and about 3" (7.5 cm) from the bottom. Using a hot dry iron, press the stencil onto the fabric for a few seconds. The wax will melt, forming a resist for the paint. Place the single balloon stencil near the opposite corner (about 6" [15 cm] from the right side and about 4½" [11.5 cm] from the top, or as desired) and repeat pressing.

6 Take your paintbrush and dab a light layer of paint over the stencil balloon shapes, working from the outer edge in. Let dry. You may need several light coats of paint until you

are satisfied with the saturation. Let dry completely.

7 Rip away the freezer paper and heat-set the paint according to the manufacturer's specifications.

8 Outline each balloon with embroidery thread (use just one or two strands), using a small running stitch (see Sewing Basics). Using a ruler and a fabric marker, draw in balloon "strings" extending to the edge of the fabric and embroider them using a running stitch as before. Draw a free-form balloon string from the remaining balloon (on the opposite corner), about 3" (7.5 cm) long or as desired and embroider with a running stitch as before.

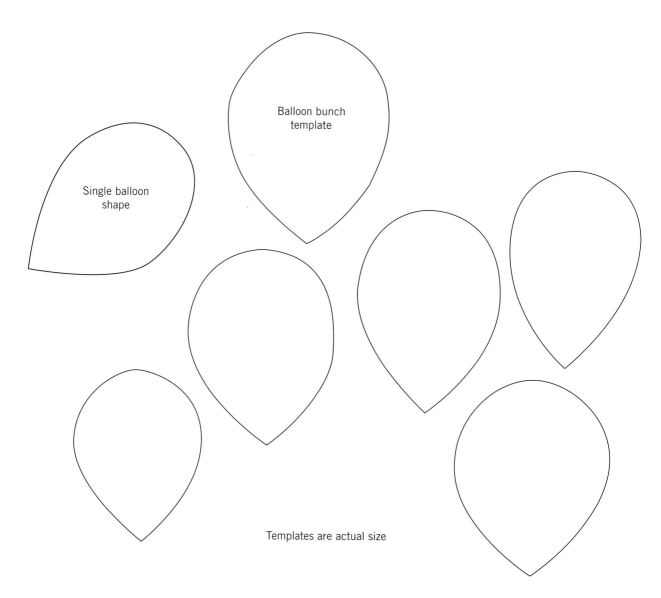

Single balloon shape

Balloon bunch template

Templates are actual size

Assemble piping and attach to pillow front

9 If you are using ready-made bias tape, skip to Step 10. Cut 1¾" (4.5 cm) wide bias strips and sew them together end to end (placing them right sides together and sewing diagonal seams) until you have a 2½ yd (2.3 m) length. (See illustration of sewing diagonal seams on page 55.) To achieve the look of the piping on my pillow, cut strips of varying lengths from the two different prints and stitch together. Trim the excess fabric from the seam allowances and press flat.

10 If you are using ready-made bias tape, press it flat. With wrong sides together, cover the upholstery piping cord with the bias tape by placing cord in the center of the bias tape and then bringing the raw edges together, enclosing the cord inside the bias tape. Pin along the length as you go to secure. Stitch the piping closed, about ⅛" (3mm) from the raw edge.

11 With the right side of the pillow front facing up, pin the raw edge of the piping to the raw edge of the pillow front.

12 Pin the beginning and the end of the piping overlapping at a 45-degree angle (**figure 1**). Baste the piping to the pillow front ⅛" (3 mm) from the raw edge. Remove the pins.

Assemble pillow back

13 With the wrong sides facing up, lay both back panel pieces side by side with short sides together. Fold each center edge over ½" (1.3 cm), then fold over again 1" (2.5 cm) and pin. Topstitch about ⅛" (3 mm) from the top of each fold, then topstitch again, about ⅛" (3 mm) from the outer edges, creating one finished center edge on each panel.

14 With the right sides facing up, overlap the center edges of each panel so that they create a finished back panel measuring 29" (73.5 cm) wide. Pin the panels together using two or three pins down the center.

Assemble complete pillow

15 With the right sides facing, pin the front and back panels together, taking care to make sure that the piping is still flipped inside and sandwiched between the two panels.

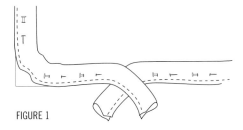

FIGURE 1

You may have to stretch the front panel slightly as you pin because the piping may have pulled it some.

16 Using a zipper foot, position the needle as close to the piping as you are able and stitch around the entire perimeter. It will make a seam allowance that is about ½" (1.3 cm) wide.

17 Trim the corner edges of the seam allowances on the back panels to match the curves on the front panel. Pink or serge the seam allowances or use the zigzag stitch on your sewing machine to finish the edges. Carefully remove all pins.

18 Turn the pillow case right-side out through the overlapped back panels and stuff with the pillow form. 🍃

See more from **MELISSA FRANTZ** at allbuttonedup.typepad.com.

Mod Pillow Pair

by Melissa Lunden

These pillows have a sophisticated style and are a great way to show off the fun details of your favorite fabrics.

Square Mod Pillow

This pillow features a white background on one side and a brown background on the opposite side. The highlighted printed fabrics are framed by the opposite fabric (brown or white, respectively).

Materials

—(18) 3" (7.5 cm) squares of different prints

—½ yd (45.5 cm) white fabric

—½ yd (45.5 cm) brown fabric

—12" (30.5 cm) invisible zipper

—14" × 14" (35.5 × 35.5 cm) pillow form or stuffing

—Invisible zipper foot

Directions

Cutting

1 From the white fabric, cut:
—9 strips 3" × ¾" (7.5 × 2 cm)
—18 strips 3¼" × ¾" (8.5 × 2 cm)
—9 strips 3½" × ¾" (9 × 2 cm)
—12 strips 3½" × 1¾" (9 × 4.5 cm)
—4 strips 14½" × 1¾" (37 × 4.5 cm)

2 From the brown fabric, cut:
—12 strips 3½" × 1¾" (9 × 4.5 cm)
—4 strips 14½" × 1¾" (37 × 4.5 cm)
—9 strips 3" × ¾" (7.5 × 2 cm)
—18 strips 3¼" × ¾" (8.5 × 2 cm)
—9 strips 3½" × ¾" (9 × 2 cm)

Piecing

Note: Use a ¼" (6 mm) seam allowance for the following steps.

3 Frame half of the 3" (7.5 cm) print squares with white fabric: sew a 3" × ¾" (7.5 × 2 cm) white strip to the top of the 3" (7.5 cm) square. Moving clockwise, add a 3¼" × ¾" (8.5 × 2 cm) white strip. Rotate to the next side and add another 3¼" × ¾" (8.5 × 2 cm) piece. Sew a 3½" × ¾" (9 × 2 cm) white strip to the final side of the square.

4 Sew a 3½" × 1¾" (9 × 4.5 cm) piece of brown fabric to the top of each square.

5 Arrange the pieces with 3 squares across and 3 down. Sew the columns and add a 3½" × 1¾" (9 × 4.5 cm) brown piece to the bottom of each column.

6 Sew a brown 14½" × 1¾" (37 × 4.5 cm) strip to the right side of each column. Sew the remaining 14½" (37 cm) piece to the left of the left column. Sew all 3 columns together.

7 Repeat these steps for the second side, switching to the brown frames/white border.

Note: Use a ½" (1.3 cm) seam allowance for the remaining steps.

8 Insert the zipper using an invisible zipper foot. Sew from the end of the zipper to the corner.

9 Sew the other 3 sides of the pillow together. Trim the corners and turn the pillow right-side out.

10 Insert a pillow form or stuffing.

Rectangular Mod Pillow

Since each fussy-cut fabric piece will be a unique size, these instructions are designed to help you re-create the look of my pillow using your favorite prints. Each side of the pillow is made up of 4 panels, and each panel consists of a fussy-cut piece framed by white fabric on all 4 sides. The fussy-cut pieces can be shifted up, down, or slightly off center by adjusting the height and width of the surrounding white pieces. To have the fussy-cut piece higher, make the top white piece shorter than the bottom. To make the fussy-cut piece placed slightly to the left of the panel center, have the left side piece narrower than the right side piece.

Materials

—8 fussy-cut prints (approximately 3"–4" (7.5–10 cm) squares and/or rectangles)

—½ yd (45.5 cm) of white fabric

—14" (35.5 cm) invisible zipper

—Invisible zipper foot

—12" × 16" (30.5 × 40.5 cm) pillow form or stuffing

11 Design the 4 panels for the pillow front and the 4 panels for the pillow back by planning for each panel to be 13" (33 cm) high and approximately 4½" (11.5 cm) wide. (The 13" [33 cm] height includes a ½" [1.3 cm] seam allowance for the top and bottom of the pillow side.) It is helpful to design each panel oversized, so that you can later trim it to the exact 13" (33 cm) height and appropriate width.

Note: When designing your panels, plan to use a ¼" (6 mm) seam allowance for the basic patchwork seams, but plan to use a ½" (1.3 cm) seam allowance when sewing the pillow front to the pillow back. (Remember to allow for a ½" [1.3 cm] seam allowance on the far right and far left panels for sewing the pillow sides together.)

12 For each panel, start by sewing a narrow white strip to each side of the selected fussy-cut fabric. (You can cut the white strips slightly longer than necessary and then trim the ends of the white strips so they're even with the top and bottom of the print fabric.) In the same manner, add a white rectangle to the top and bottom of each print/white rectangle. Trim each panel so it's 13" (33 cm) high.

13 Sew the 4 panels together. It should measure 17" (43 cm) wide. (If your piece is too wide, you can trim white fabric from the far sides, or you can increase the size of the seam allowances between the panels. If your piece is not the full 17" [43 cm], just add a white strip to 1 or both edges.) Repeat for the opposite side of the pillow.

14 Trim the invisible zipper to 12" (30.5 cm) and iron the coils open.

15 Center the zipper in the middle of the pieced front and back, and insert it using an invisible zipper foot. Then sew from the zipper to the corner with a ½" (1.3 cm) seam allowance.

16 With a ½" (1.3 cm) seam allowance, sew the other 3 sides of the pillow together. Trim the corners and turn the pillow right-side out. Insert a pillow form or stuffing. ✐

Visit **MELISSA LUNDEN'S** website at lundendesigns.blogspot.com.

Materials

—1 yd (91.5 cm) of 54" (137 cm) wide home decorator print fabric for piecing and side strips (Main)

—¾ yd (68.5 cm) of 54" (137 cm) wide coordinating home decorator print fabric for piecing (Contrast)

—Pattern tracing cloth or tracing paper

—Coordinating sewing thread

—Polyester fiberfill

—Size 8 pearl cotton in color to coordinate with fabrics

—Eight ¾" (19 mm) coverable buttons with tool (usually available together)

—Waxed button thread

—Handsewing needle

—6" (15 cm) upholstery needle

—Tailor's chalk (optional)

—Long clear ruler (optional)

Finished Size
20" × 20" × 5" (51 × 51 × 12.5 cm)

----

notes

✽ All seam allowances are ½" (1.3 cm) unless otherwise noted.

✽ For explanations of terms and techniques, see Sewing Basics.

✽ Sew all seams with right sides together.

✽ If desired, use tailor's chalk and a clear gridded acrylic ruler to draw lines 1" (2.5 cm) from the long raw edges of the triangle and side pieces before assembling the pillow, to use as guides for the self-welting stitches.

✽ Use waxed button thread, upholstery thread, or other heavy thread to attach the buttons securely.

Tufted Floor Pillow
by Carol Zentgraf

Add some fashionable extra seating to any room with this comfy floor pillow. Choose two graphic home décor prints for the simple fabric piecing. The center is tufted and the edges are stitched into a self-welting as finishing touches.

Directions

Make the pattern and cut the fabric

1 Draw a 20" × 20" (51 × 51 cm) square on the pattern tracing cloth or tracing paper. Draw diagonal lines across the square from corner to corner, creating four triangles. Add ½" (1.3 cm) seam allowances to all three sides (**figure 1**) of one triangle only; cut out this triangle along the outer lines. This is the triangle pattern for piecing.

2 From the Main fabric, cut:
—Four triangles, using the triangle pattern
—Four 6" × 21" (15 × 53.5 cm) side strips
—Eight circles, using pattern on coverable button package

3 From the Contrast fabric, cut:
—Four triangles, using the triangle pattern

Assemble the pillow

4 Arrange two triangles from each fabric into a square with alternating colors. Sew the triangles into two pairs, then sew the pairs together to make the pillow top, keeping the fabric arrangement intact. Press the seams open. Repeat to make the pillow bottom.

5 Sew the short ends of the side strips together, beginning and ending the stitching ½" (1.3 cm) from the long edges, and leaving a 3" (7.5 cm) opening in one seam. Press the seam allowances open, pressing the seam allowances under along the opening in the seam.

6 Sew the side strips to the pillow top, matching the side seams with the corners. Repeat to sew the side strips to the pillow bottom. Turn

right-side out through the gap in the seam and press.

7 Stuff the pillow with polyester fiberfill. Slip-stitch the opening in the side strip closed.

Finishing the pillow

8 Thread the upholstery needle with a long length of pearl cotton and knot one end. To make the welting around the top edge, make large running stitches around the pillow, working from the side panel to the pillow top and trapping some stuffing in the welt. Begin by inserting the needle in a corner seam and bringing it to the right side of the side panel, ½" (1.3 cm) from the seam that joins the side to the pillow top. Tug the thread to bury the knot inside the pillow. Insert the needle ½" (1.3 cm) away, still ½" (1.3 cm) from the seam, so it emerges on the pillow top ½" (1.3 cm) from the seam. Make another ½" (1.3 cm) stitch, taking the needle back to the side panel. Continue stitching in this manner around the top edge of the pillow, pulling the thread tightly every few stitches to create the ½" (1.3 cm) wide self-welting **(figure 2)**. End one thread and begin another by burying the knots inside the pillow. Repeat

the entire step to create self-welting around the bottom edge.

9 Follow the manufacturer's instructions to cover the buttons with fabric. On each side of the pillow, make marks on each diagonal seam line 3" (7.5 cm) from the center. Cut an 18" (45.5 cm) length of the waxed button thread and slide one button shank onto the center of the thread. Insert both thread ends through the eye of the upholstery needle. Stitch through the pillow at one mark on the top, bringing the needle out at the corresponding mark on the bottom. Remove the needle and slide a button shank onto one thread end. Tie the thread ends together under the button, pulling tautly to create a tuft. Knot the threads several times and trim the ends even with the underside of the button. Repeat to add the three remaining buttons. 🍃

CAROL ZENTGRAF is the author of *Pillows, Cushions and Tuffets*; *Decorative Storage*; *The Well-Dressed Window*; *Machine Embroidery Room-by-Room*; *Sewing for Outdoor Spaces*; and *Sewing Christmas Greetings*.

FIGURE 1

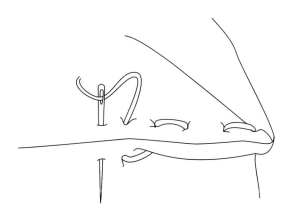

FIGURE 2

Materials

—½ yd (45.5 cm) (total) of assorted cottons and linens in cool colors, such as blue, green, and purple

—½ yd (45.5 cm) (total) of assorted cottons and linens in warm colors, such as red, yellow, and orange

—¾ yd (68.5 cm) of cotton muslin

—¾ yd (68.5 cm) of graphic print for backing

—¼ yd (23 cm) of coordinating graphic print for binding

—8½ × 11" (A4; 21.5 × 28 cm) paper

—All-purpose sewing thread

—Machine quilting thread

—25" (63.5 cm) square of cotton batting

—20" (51 cm) zipper

—20" × 20" (51 × 51 cm) pillow form

—Quilter's acrylic ruler

—Rotary cutter and self-healing mat

—Quilt basting materials

—Zipper foot

Finished Size
20 × 20" (51 × 51 cm)

---

notes

* All seam allowances are ¼" (6 mm) unless otherwise noted.

* The fabric for the top is cut freehand. You do not need to use measuring tools to cut the squares and strips. You'll be amazed at how well you can eye the sizes you need. Allow yourself the liberty of cutting fabric the way you would draw with a pencil.

Tuesday Pillow
by Malka Dubrawsky

This quilted pillow is bold and bright due to the wonkiness of the blocks and the colorful fabric combo. The improvisational design can be made with a mix of freehand cutting and a fun and fearless approach to color.

Directions
Cut out fabric

1 From the cool colors, freehand cut nine squares ranging in size from about 2" (5 cm) to 4" (10 cm) square.

2 From the cool colors, freehand cut at least 40 strips in widths varying from 1" (2.5 cm) to 3" (7.5 cm) and no longer than 9" (23 cm).

3 From the warm colors, freehand cut at least 40 strips in widths varying from 1" (2.5 cm) to 3" (7.5 cm) and no longer than 9" (23 cm).

4 From the muslin, measure and cut a 25" (63.5 cm) square.

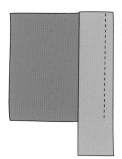

A Sew a strip to the center square.

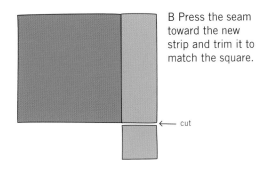

B Press the seam toward the new strip and trim it to match the square.

← cut

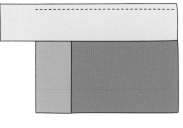

C Attach the next strip to an adjacent edge.

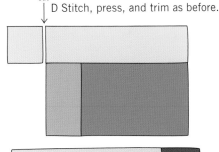

cut

D Stitch, press, and trim as before.

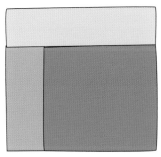

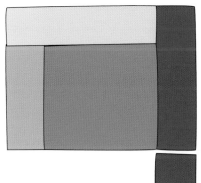

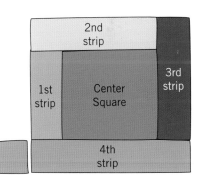

2nd strip

1st strip

Center Square

3rd strip

4th strip

5 From the backing fabric, measure and cut two 20½ × 15" (52 × 38 cm) rectangles.

6 From the binding fabric measure and cut three binding strips 2" (5 cm) wide across the fabric width.

Make blocks

Note: You'll be creating a 7¼" (18.5 cm) square template either to use as a guide or to square off each block as you make it. If you elect to use the template as a guide, you'll want to square off the completed pillow top so that it measures 20½ × 20½" (52 cm × 52 cm) before assembling the pillow. See illustrations above for help with block construction.

7 Measure and cut a 7¼" (18.5 cm) square template from the 8½ × 11" (A4; 21.5 × 28 cm) paper.

8 Each pieced square begins with a center square in a cool color. Place a cool-colored strip along one edge of a center square, right sides together and raw edges matched, and stitch the two together.

9 Press the seam toward the new strip. If the strip is longer than the square, trim it so they are the same length.

10 Place a second cool-colored strip, right sides together, along an adjacent side of the center square. The new strip will cross both the center square and one end of the previous strip. Work clockwise or

counterclockwise around the center square but be consistent throughout the block.

11 Sew the new strip to the first two pieces. Press the seam toward the new strip and trim as before.

12 Lay a warm-colored strip on the pieced unit, right sides together and raw edges matched, along the side formed by the center square and the second strip.

13 Sew, press, and trim as before.

14 Continue around the center square, placing a warm-colored strip along the edge formed by the center square and the ends of the first

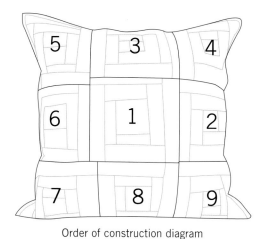

Order of construction diagram

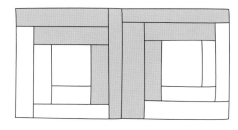

FIGURE 1

and third strips. Sew, press, and trim as before.

15 Repeat the steps above, alternating two cool-colored strips with two warm-colored strips, until the block is at least 7¼" (18.5 cm) square. *Note:* The number of strips needed will vary depending on the size of the center square and the widths of the strips.

16 If you're squaring off individual blocks, lay the template piece on top of a completed block and trim to fit.

17 If you're not squaring off individual blocks, proceed to making a second block and add or delete fabric so that the blocks are the same size.

18 Repeat Steps 8–17 to make eight more blocks.

Assemble top

Note: To assemble the blocks in the intended order, refer to the order of construction diagram above of the finished pillow. All seams are sewn with the blocks right sides together.

19 Place blocks 1 and 2 right sides together, matching two warm-colored edges. Check to ensure that the two blocks will create a warm-colored "T" when the edges are seamed, and rotate one or both blocks if necessary. Stitch the seam and press it toward block 1 (**figure 1**).

20 Place blocks 3 and 4 right sides together, matching two warm-colored edges so the two blocks form

a warm-colored inverted "T" shape. Stitch the seam and press it toward block 4.

21 Pin sewn blocks 1 and 2 to sewn blocks 3 and 4 along the long edge of warm-colored strips. Stitch together. Press the seam toward blocks 1 and 2. Set aside.

22 Place blocks 5 and 6 side by side with the warm-colored strips positioned along the bottom left edge of block 5 and the top left edge of block 6. Keeping the blocks oriented, sew blocks 5 and 6 together. Press the seam toward block 5.

23 Referring to the schematic, pin sewn blocks 5 and 6 to the previously sewn foursome. Stitch together and press the seam toward blocks 1 and 3.

24 Place blocks 7 and 8 side by side with the cool-colored strips positioned along the upper right-hand corner of block 7 and the upper left-hand corner of block 8. Stitch the blocks together, pressing the seam toward block 7.

25 Pin block 9 to sewn blocks 7 and 8 so the warm-colored strips meet along the bottom right corner of block 8 and the bottom left corner of block 9.

26 Stitch together, pressing the seam toward block 8.

27 Pin the two parts of the pillow top, right sides together, along one long edge (as shown in the schematic). Stitch together, then press the seam toward blocks 7, 8, and 9.

Note: If you've elected to square off the pillow top once it's constructed, do so now.

Quilt pillow top

28 Lay the muslin square, wrong-side up, on a flat surface. Layer the batting and pillow top, right-side up, on the muslin.

29 Baste the layers together with safety pins or by hand with needle and thread.

30 Set the machine for free motion quilting and quilt the pillow top with concentric squares in every block. Trim the layers so they are flush.

Finish pillow

31 Lay one of the backing pieces, wrong-side up, on the ironing board. Press ¼" (6 mm) to the wrong side along one 20½" (52 cm) edge.

32 Press an additional 1¼" (3 cm) toward the wrong side on the same edge.

33 Lay the zipper right-side down along the pressed edge, making sure that the zipper tape edge is flush with the ¼" (6 mm) fold (see **figure 4** of Pi Pillow on page 31). Pin the zipper in place.

34 Using a zipper foot, stitch the zipper to the backing piece ⅛" (3 mm) from the pressed edge (see **figure 5** of Pi Pillow).

35 Lay the second backing piece, wrong-side up, on the ironing

Binding Instructions

1. Sew the binding strips together using diagonal seams **(figure 1)**. Trim the excess fabric as shown, leaving ¼" (6 mm) seam allowance, and press the seams open. Fold the binding in half lengthwise, with wrong sides together, and press. The pressed strip will form a double thickness binding around the pillow top.

2. Position the binding on the pillow top with raw edges matched. Begin sewing about 3" (7.5 cm) before a corner and leave about 6" (15 cm) of the binding fabric free at the beginning.

3. Sew through all layers to the point where the seam lines meet at the corner **(figure 2)**, backstitch, and cut the threads.

4. Rotate the pillow 90° to position it for sewing the next side. Fold the binding fabric up, away from the pillow, at a 45° angle **(figure 3)**, then fold it back down along the pillow raw edge **(figure 4)**. This forms a miter at the corner.

5. Stitch the second side, beginning at the raw edge and ending at the next corner's seam line juncture. Repeat the steps for mitering.

6. Continue around the pillow form. After completing the fourth corner, stitch about 3" (7.5 cm) more, backstitch, and cut the threads.

7. Unfold the binding ends and trim the excess length so the binding fits neatly along the remaining pillow edge, leaving ½" (1.3 cm) overlap for seam allowances. Join the ends with a diagonal seam **(figure 1)** and finger-press the seam open. Refold the binding along the lengthwise crease and finish stitching the binding to the pillow.

8. Fold the binding over the pillow raw edges to the pillow back. Match the binding's lengthwise fold to the seam line and slip-stitch the binding in place, covering the pillow raw edges.

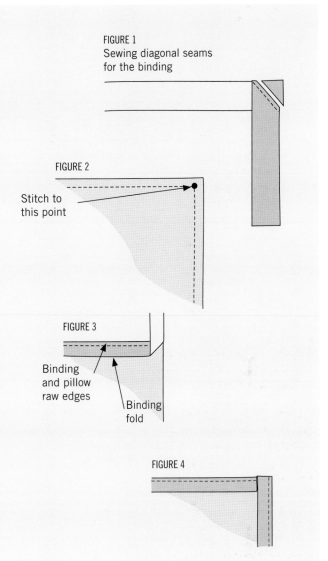

FIGURE 1
Sewing diagonal seams for the binding

FIGURE 2
Stitch to this point

FIGURE 3
Binding and pillow raw edges

Binding fold

FIGURE 4

---

board. Press ¼" (6 mm) to the wrong side along one 20½" (52 cm) edge.

36 Working on a flat surface, place half of backing with zipper already attached so that the right side is facing up. Fold back the edge that covers the zipper. Pin the second backing piece, right side facing up, so that the pressed edge abuts the zipper teeth along the unstitched edge. Stitch the second backing piece to the zipper tape, stitching close to the pressed fold.

37 Lay the assembled backing right-side down on a flat surface. Lay the quilted pillow top, right-side up, on top of the backing and pin together. Trim excess backing. Set aside.

38 Sew the binding strips together using diagonal seams (see Binding Instructions above).

39 Sew the binding strips to the pinned pillow and backing, encasing the raw edges.

40 Insert the pillow form. 🍃

MALKA DUBRAWSKY is the author of *Fresh Quilting* and blogs at stitchindye .blogspot.com.

Back of pillow

Pi Pillow

by Malka Dubrawsky

Inspired by pie and pi, this pillow top is constructed out of wedges, and the parts come together to form a perfect circle. Created with sweet and simple graphic prints, the pillow's roundness is emphasized by quilted lines that run in a concentric circle from the center and accented by a little ruffle around the edges.

Materials

—Scraps of 16 assorted cotton prints

—½ yd (45.5 cm) of 45" (114.5 cm) wide
coordinating fabric for backing

—½ yd (45.5 cm) of 45" (114.5 cm) wide
coordinating print for ruffle

—Three 18" (45.5 cm) square pieces of cotton muslin

—All-purpose sewing thread

—Machine quilting thread

—16" (40.5 cm) zipper

—12 oz (340 g) of polyester stuffing

—18" (45.5 cm) square of cotton batting

—Pi template on page 32

—Quilt basting materials

—Zipper foot

—Fabric marking pen

—Rotary cutter and self-healing mat

Finished Size

14" (35.5 cm) diameter

------

note

✳ All seam allowances are ¼" (6 mm) unless otherwise noted.

Directions

Cut out fabric

1 Using the Pi template, cut 16 wedges from the cotton prints.

2 Cut two pieces measuring 16" × 10" (40.5 × 25.5 cm) from the backing fabric.

3 From ruffle fabric, cut bias strips measuring 1¼" (3.2 cm) wide and totaling about 44" (112 cm) in length. To cut bias strips, begin by folding one selvedge edge to meet the crosswise edge (figure 1). Cut along the fold; the resulting edge lies on the bias. Cut strips parallel to the bias edge, measuring each one's length through the center, until the strips total 44" (112 cm) or more (figure 2).

Make pillow top

4 Pin two wedge pieces right sides together and sew along one long edge. Press the seam open.

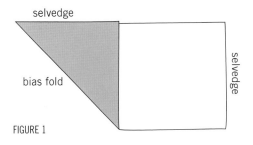

FIGURE 1

selvedge

bias fold

FIGURE 1

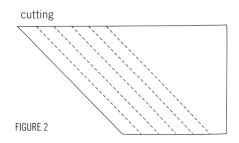

cutting

selvedge

FIGURE 2

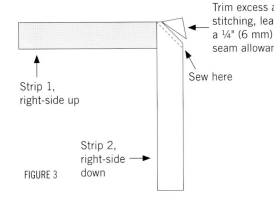

Strip 1,
right-side up

Trim excess after
stitching, leaving
a ¼" (6 mm)
seam allowance.

Sew here

Strip 2,
right-side →
down

FIGURE 3

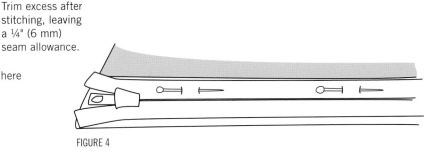

FIGURE 4

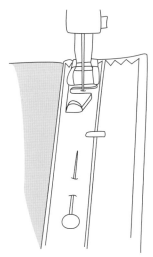

FIGURE 5

5 Pin a third wedge piece to the pair, right sides together, and sew. Press the seam open.

6 Continue to add wedge pieces, pressing the seams open, until you have a half circle constructed from eight wedges.

7 Repeat Steps 4–6 with the remaining wedges.

8 Pin both half circles, right sides together, and sew along the straight edge. Press the seam open.

Quilt pillow top

9 Lay one muslin square on a flat surface, wrong-side up. Layer the batting and the pillow top, right sides up, on top of the backing.

10 Baste the layers together with safety pins or baste by hand with needle and thread.

11 Set the machine to allow for free-motion stitching (drop the feed dogs and use a darning foot). Machine-quilt the top, starting in the center and working outward in concentric circles about ¼" (6 mm) apart.

12 Trim the muslin and batting to match the pieced pillow top.

Make the ruffle

13 Sew the ruffle strips into one length using diagonal seams

(**figure 3**). Fold the ruffle in half, lengthwise, with wrong sides together, and press, being careful not to stretch the bias fabric.

14 Pin the ruffle to the pillow top, right sides together and raw edges matched, beginning with a diagonally cut end. When the ruffle is pinned all around the pillow, carefully mark the bias strip where it meets the beginning of the strip.

15 Unpin a few inches of the ruffle to provide working room. Add ½" (1.3 cm) to the end for seam allowances and cut the bias strip on the diagonal. Join the beginning and end with a ¼" (6 mm) diagonal seam. Press the seam open, then refold the bias strip and repin to the pillow top.

16 Sew the ruffle to the pillow top a scant ¼" (6 mm) from the raw edge.

Finish the pillow

17 Lay one of the backing pieces, wrong-side up, on the ironing board. Press ¼" (6 mm) to the wrong side along one 16" (40.5 cm) edge. Press an additional 1¼" (3.2 cm) toward the wrong side on the same edge.

18 Lay the zipper right-side down along the pressed edge, making

sure that the zipper tape edge is flush with the ¼" (6 mm) pressed edge (**figure 4**). Pin the zipper in place.

19 Using a zipper foot, stitch the zipper to the backing piece, ⅛" (3 mm) from the pressed edge (**figure 5**).

20 Lay the second backing piece, wrong-side up, on the ironing board. Press ¼" (6 mm) toward the wrong side along one 16" (40.5 cm) edge.

21 Working on a flat surface, place half of backing with zipper already attached so that the right

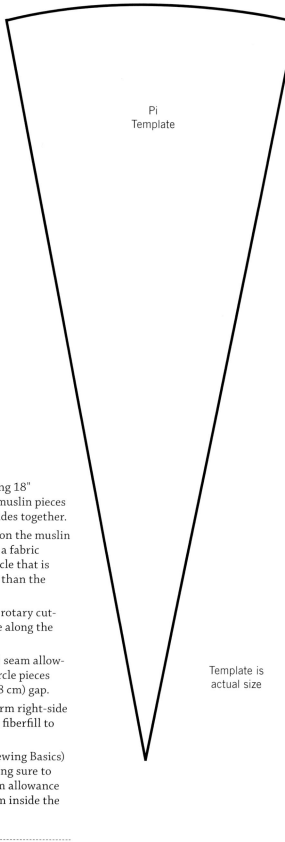

Pi
Template

Template is
actual size

side is facing up. Fold back the edge that covers the zipper. Pin the second backing piece, right side facing up, so that the pressed edge abuts the zipper teeth along the unstitched edge. Stitch the second backing piece to the zipper tape, stitching close to the pressed fold.

22 Lay the assembled backing right-side up on a flat surface. Place the pillow top right-side down on the backing, making sure that the edge with the zipper pull meets and is perpendicular to the pillow edge. *Note:* Leave the zipper slightly open to ease turning the finished pillow right-side out.

23 Pin the pillow top to the backing and trim the backing and zipper tapes to match the pillow front. *Note:* When trimming excess parts of the zipper, keep the zipper mostly closed and trim the end opposite the zipper pull.

24 Using a ¼" (6 mm) seam allowance, sew the pillow backing to the top.

25 Turn the finished pillow right-side out. Press the edges out so they are crisp.

Make pillow form

26 Place the remaining 18" (45.5 cm) square muslin pieces on a flat surface, right sides together.

27 Center the pillow on the muslin squares, and with a fabric marking pen, mark a circle that is about ½" (1.3 cm) larger than the pillow.

28 With scissors or a rotary cutter, cut out a circle along the marked line.

29 Using a ¼" (6 mm) seam allowance, stitch the circle pieces together, leaving a 7" (18 cm) gap.

30 Turn the pillow form right-side out and stuff with fiberfill to the desired firmness.

31 Whipstitch (see Sewing Basics) the gap closed, being sure to turn in a ¼" (6 mm) seam allowance at the gap. Place the form inside the pillow cover. 🍃

MALKA DUBRAWSKY is the author of *Fresh Quilting* and blogs at stitchindye .blogspot.com.

DECORATIVE BED PILLOWS

Serenity Sham

by Donna Babylon

A bedroom isn't complete without a profusion of pillows.
Decorate your pillows with this easy-to-make sham!

Materials

—The pillow sham directions are for
a standard 20" × 26" (51 × 66 cm)
pillow.

—1⅞ yd (1.7 m) fabric 1 (top, bottom,
and backing)

—¼ yd (23 cm) fabric 2 (accent bands)

—¼ yd (23 cm) fabric 3 (center)

—1 yd (91.5 cm) fleece batting

----

note

✱ Use ½" (1.3 cm) wide seam
allowances.

Directions

Cut the fabric

Fabric 1 (top strip, bottom strip, and back):

—2 strips 9½" × 33" (24 × 84 cm)

—1 rectangle 29" × 31½" (73.5 × 80 cm; back)

—1 rectangle 13½" × 29" (34.5 × 73.5 cm; back)

Fabric 2 (accent bands):

—2 strips 2½" × 33" (6.5 × 84 cm)

Fabric 3 (center):

—1 strip 7" × 33" (18 × 84 cm)

Lining:

—29" × 33" (73.5 × 84 cm)

Batting:

—29" × 33" (73.5 × 84 cm)

Construction

1 Assemble the sham front by piecing the 33" (84 cm) strips in this order: fabric 1, fabric 2, fabric 3, fabric 2, and then fabric 1. Press the seams toward the darkest fabrics.

2 Place the batting against the wrong side of the sham front. Directly on top of the batting, place the lining; all raw edges should be even. Machine baste around the edge to hold the layers.

3 Hem each inside edge of the back pieces with a double 2" (5 cm) hem.

4 With right sides together, pin the sham backs to the sham front. Overlap the 2 back pieces so the outside edges are even with the sham front.

5 Stitch around all edges of the sham. To eliminate bulk, trim the corner seam allowances diagonally. Zigzag or serge the seam allowances together.

6 Turn the sham right–side out. For sharp corners, use a point turner to gently push the fabric out from the inside. Press the seam.

7 To form the flange, topstitch all around the sham, 3" (7.5 cm) from the edge. Insert the pillow through the back opening. 🍃

Visit **DONNA BABYLON'S** website at moresplashthancash.com.

Reverse Appliqué Pillow
by Kevin Kosbab

Break through the plaid grid with a swatch of contrasting fabric and free-form topstitching to give a classic pillow a modern touch of embellishment. Combining classic wool plaid with a bright cotton print makes a fresh color statement.

Materials

—½ yd (45.5 cm) of 45" (114.5 cm) wide wool plaid for pillow front (Main)

—5" × 5" (12.5 × 12.5 cm) scrap of cotton print (Contrast; see Notes)

—½ yd (45.5 cm) of 45" (114.5 cm) wide coordinating cotton print for pillow back (Back)

—Wool-acrylic blend thread, such as Madeira Lana, in three or more shades of a color complementary to Contrast fabric

—Coordinating sewing thread

—16" × 16" (40.5 × 40.5 cm) pillow form

—Pinking shears

—Point turner or similar tool such as a chopstick

Finished Size

16" × 16" (40.5 × 40.5 cm)

notes

✳ All seam allowances are ½" (1.3 cm) unless otherwise noted.

✳ For explanations of terms and techniques, see Sewing Basics.

✳ Feel free to alter the size of your Contrast square to suit the scale of the bars in your plaid.

✳ Using cotton for the pillow back conserves more expensive wool and adds design detail, but the back panels could be made from Main fabric, too.

✳ Other threads would work for the stitch embellishment; the sample uses a wool-blend thread that held its own against the wool fabric. The combination of wool thread and fabric makes a lot of lint, so clean your machine frequently.

✳ The intersecting topstitching that will be cut out of the front panel has an interesting look. If you cut the square out carefully, you could use the fabric to make a coordinated covered-button closure for the back panels of the pillow.

Directions

Cut the fabric

1 Cut one 16" × 16" (40.5 × 40.5 cm) pillow front from the Main fabric with the bars of the plaid evenly spaced (bars should appear equi-distant from the outer edges of the square). One of the squares where perpendicular bars cross will be cut out to reveal the Contrast fabric, so consider where this will be placed when planning the front panel's placement on the fabric.

2 Cut two 11" × 16" (28 × 40.5 cm) pillow back panels from the Back fabric.

Embellish the pillow front

3 Using the wool-blend thread, topstitch up and down over the square that will be cut out, extend-ing the stitching lines well beyond the square. At the end of each line, leave the needle in the fabric, lift the presser foot, pivot the fabric to make a return stitching line, lower the presser foot, and continue to sew (figure 1). Angle each line slightly, pivoting at different distances from the center to vary the appearance. Change thread colors periodically to add depth to the stitching.

4 Topstitch back and forth over the square to be cut out, perpendicu-lar to the stitching in Step 3, follow-ing the same method (figure 2).

5 Pink the edges of the Contrast fabric, leaving a 4" (10 cm) square. Baste the Contrast scrap to the back of the embellished front panel, directly behind the central part of the topstitching where the perpendicular lines cross, with the right side of the Contrast fabric against the wrong side of the front panel.

6 With the front panel right-side up, topstitch a rough square through both layers of fabric, inside the line of basting stitches. Sew around this square a few times, varying the stitch path with each repetition, using two or more thread colors. As well as being decorative, these stitches will hold the Contrast fabric in place.

7 Remove the basting stitches. Carefully snip into the Main fabric inside the sewn square, slipping the scissors point between the Main and Contrast fabrics. Cut away the Main fabric inside the sewn square to reveal the Contrast fabric behind, being very careful not to cut through the Contrast fabric. Roughen the cut edges—the topstitching will keep fraying from traveling beyond the square.

Finish the pillow

8 Fold ½" (1.3 cm) to the wrong side along a 16" (40.5 cm) edge of one back panel and press. Fold an additional ½" (1.3 cm) to the wrong side along the same edge and press again. Repeat with the remaining back panel. Sew each hem closed near the inner fold.

9 With right sides together and raw edges aligned, pin the pillow front and the back panels together. The hemmed edges of the back panels will overlap at the center. Sew all around the perimeter.

10 Trim the corners diagonally to reduce bulk, pink the raw edges, and turn the cover right-side out, gently working the corners out with a point turner or similar tool. Insert the pillow form through the opening. 🍃

KEVIN KOSBAB regularly designs modern quilts and sewing projects for *Stitch* and other magazines. Find his *Feed Dog Designs* patterns in stores and on the Web at feeddog.net.

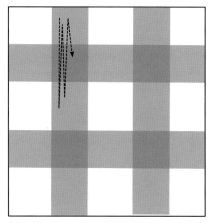

FIGURE 1

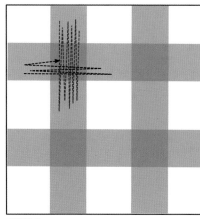

FIGURE 2

Cute-as-a-Button Pillow
by Tricia Waddell

Layer small coordinating buttons for a modern detail that turns a plain linen pillow into a stylish room accent. Add simple knife pleats and a tea-dyed background for the buttons and then stuff it with 100% cotton filling.

Materials
—¾ yd (68 cm) of medium-weight linen for main pillow fabric

—½ yd (45.5 cm) of medium-weight linen in a contrasting color

Other Supplies
—Various buttons in coordinating shades (scrapbooking stores are a great place to find packs of small coordinating buttons)

—All-purpose thread to match main fabric

—100% cotton stuffing

—Clear acrylic ruler

—Tailor's chalk or fabric pencil

—10" (25.5 cm) diameter embroidery hoop (optional)

—Handsewing needle

—Pressing cloth

Finished Size
11" × 18" (28 × 45.5 cm)

---

notes

* All seam allowances are ½" (1.3 cm) unless otherwise noted.

* Can't find the perfect natural shade of linen? Try tea dyeing. Brew two cups of tea, let the tea steep for a couple of minutes, then soak a piece of white linen in it for 5 to 10 minutes. Ta-da! The perfect sepia-toned shade of linen to match the buttons. Try the same idea with fruity herbal teas for varying colors.

Directions

Cut out fabric

1 Cut a 12" × 34½" (30.5 × 87.5 cm) piece from the main fabric for the pillow front. Cut a 12" × 19" (30.5 × 48.5 cm) piece from the main fabric for the pillow back.

Create button detail

2 Using the clear acrylic ruler, mark a 5¾ × 7¾" (14.5 × 19.5 cm) rectangle on the contrasting fabric with a fabric pencil (do not mark this along the edge of the fabric; leave enough fabric around the rectangle to secure the fabric in the 10" [25.5 cm] embroidery hoop). Along one short side, mark a line ½" (1.3 cm) inside the rectangle (running all the way along and parallel to the edge. On the remaining three sides, mark a line ¼" (6 mm) inside the rectangle as before. These are your seam allowances.

3 To make it easier to sew on all the buttons, put the contrasting fabric in an embroidery hoop with the drawn rectangle evenly centered. Be careful not to pull the fabric too tightly in the hoop to avoid puckering.

4 With a handsewing needle and thread, begin sewing your buttons in the center of the rectangle, keeping them at least ½" (1.3 cm) away from the seam allowance lines. Layer the buttons as you go, randomly distributing button sizes and colors.

5 When you are finished sewing buttons, cut the fabric to the size of the outside rectangle markings. Fold under the three ¼" (6 mm) seam allowances and press. Set aside.

Create knife pleats

6 Place your larger pillow front fabric right-side up, and starting from one short end, mark a line 1½" (3.8 cm) from the edge (running all the way along and parallel to the short edge). Mark 22 more lines, each 1" (2.5 cm) apart. These will determine the size and position of your pleats.

7 Beginning at the second line (toward the middle of the fabric piece), fold the fabric over (with right sides together) along the line and finger-press, then fold it back over (with wrong sides together) along the next line (**figure 1**); secure with pins at the top, middle, and bottom of the fold. To make the next pleat, skip a line and fold the fabric over along the next line, then fold it back over along the next line (don't skip one this time); this will place the edge of your next fold along the line previously skipped so that there is 1" (2.5 cm) between the first two pleats (**figure 2**). Continue creating these "accordion" folds in the same manner, pinning at the top, middle, and bottom of each fold to secure as you go. Continue folding pleats until you have 1" (2.5 cm) left at the end. Using a pressing cloth, iron the pleated folds in place.

8 Baste (see Sewing Basics) ¼" (6 mm) from the top and bottom edges of the pillow front to secure the pleats in place.

9 With a handsewing needle and thread, tack the pleats at three evenly spaced points along each pleat to hold it in place. To tack, pick up a few threads on the underside of a pleat near the edge but far enough back to remain hidden, then pick up a few threads on the top of the opposite pleat (make sure it will still be hidden under the top pleat). Keeping the stitch slightly loose, pick up a few threads on the underside of the top pleat again, then tie off and use the needle to thread the tail through the pleat for a short distance. Bring the needle out and cut the thread against the pleat so that the tail will retreat into the fabric with a gentle tug.

Assemble pillow

10 On the pillow front piece (with right side facing), pin the button detail (right-side up) opposite the pleated side, centering the ½" (1.3 cm) seam allowance side of the detail on the short side of the pillow front and lining up the raw edges. Make sure the ¼" (6 mm) seam allowances on the button detail piece are still folded under and then topstitch (see Sewing Basics) ⅛" (3 mm) from the edge on all three sides, turning at the corners without lifting the needle for a continuous stitch line.

11 Place the pillow back fabric piece on top of the pillow front, right sides facing. Pin and then stitch around three sides of the pillow, leaving the short side with the button detail open. Clip the corners by cutting a triangle into the seam allowances at each corner with the point of the triangles pointing toward the seam; be careful not to cut through the seam or cut so closely that the fabric will fray through the seam. Turn right-side out through the opening.

12 Stuff the pillow with cotton stuffing. Be careful not to overstuff so you don't distort the pleats.

13 Fold in the remaining ½" (1.3 cm) seam allowances and handstitch the pillow closed using a slip stitch (see Sewing Basics). 🍃

TRICIA WADDELL was the founding editor of *Stitch* magazine. When she's not working, she spends her time making stuff.

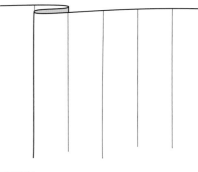

FIGURE 1

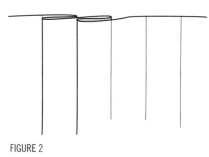

FIGURE 2

Materials

—1 yd (91.5 cm) beige burlap or other coarse, plain-weave fabric

—¼ yd (23 cm) cream cotton eyelet lace fabric (20" [51 cm] wide or wider; shown: a simple, allover pattern with lots of open space for the contrast fabric to show from underneath)

—¼ yd (23 cm) quilting-weight cotton fabric in a contrast color (shown: blue)

—1¼ yd (1.2 m) of 20" (51 cm) wide fusible interfacing

—Coordinating sewing thread

—Embroidery floss in contrasting color of your choice (shown: dark blue)

—18" (45.5 cm) square pillow form

—Disappearing-ink fabric marker

—Drinking glass or circle template, 3½" (9 cm) in diameter (for tracing circles)

—Acrylic ruler

—Embroidery needle

—Point turner (optional)

Finished Size
18" × 18" (45.5 × 45.5 cm)

notes

∗ All seam allowances are ½" (1.3 cm) unless otherwise indicated.

∗ For explanation of terms and techniques, see Sewing Basics.

∗ Burlap fabric frays easily. To stabilize the fabric, back each piece of burlap with iron-on interfacing cut to the same size. Choose a lightweight interfacing that won't impede the embroidery needle.

Directions

Cut fabric

1 Cut the following from the burlap and the interfacing:

—19" × 19" (48.5 × 48.5 cm) piece for the pillow front

—2 panels, each 19" × 12½" (48.5 × 31.5 cm) for the pillow back

—Cut a 19" × 5" (48.5 × 12.5 cm) piece from the eyelet fabric.

—Cut a 19" × 5" (48.5 × 12.5 cm) piece from the quilting cotton.

Assemble front panel

2 Using a disappearing-ink fabric marker, draw circles on the right

Modern Eyelet Pillow
by Blair Stocker

Natural burlap meets feminine eyelet in this fun pillow with an inspired texture mix. The half circles are created with reverse appliqué and accented with easy hand embroidery. A simple envelope pillow back makes it quick to assemble.

side of the front panel, one above the other, from top to bottom, using your circle template or glass. Position the circles 3½" (9 cm) from the fabric raw edge (left or right edge, whichever you prefer). Leave ¼" (6 mm) of space between circles and keep drawing them right up to and off the fabric edges at the top and bottom. Once all the circles are drawn, use a straight-edge to draw a straight line through the centers of the circles, from top to bottom, 5¼" (13.5 cm) from the raw edge (figure 1).

3 Lay the eyelet rectangle on the contrast fabric rectangle right sides up and baste the layers together, ⅛" (3 mm) from the raw edges. Pin the eyelet and contrast fabric to the front panel from behind, centering them behind the circles. Smooth all layers flat and pin together securely.

4 Using 3 strands of embroidery floss, handsew a running stitch on each drawn circle on the front pillow panel. Be sure to catch all the layers while stitching; use a stabbing motion with the needle, rather than a rocking motion, if necessary. Stitch along the straight line dividing each circle in half, but do not sew between the circles. Remove the marks, following the pen manufacturer's instructions.

5 Using small, sharp scissors such as embroidery scissors, carefully cut through the burlap only over one half of each circle, cutting ¼" (6 mm) inside the embroidered stitch lines. Alternate which half of each circle you cut to create a pattern (see photos). This exposes the eyelet with the contrast fabric peeking through it.

Finish pillow

6 To hem the back panels of the pillow, fold ½" (1.3 cm) to the wrong side along one 19" (48.5 cm) edge of each piece and press, then fold over another ½" (1.3 cm) on the same edge and press again. Hem each panel with a straight stitch, stitching close to the folded edge and using matching thread.

7 Lay the panels on your work surface in this order: back panels (right-side up and with hems overlapping in center), front panel (wrong-side up and with circle

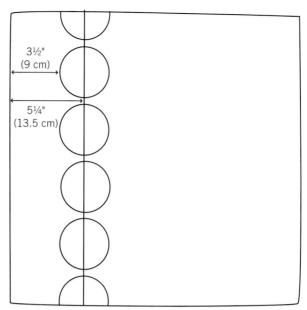

FIGURE 1

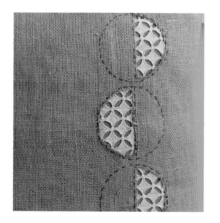
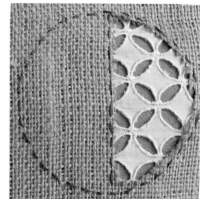

pattern running from top to bottom). Match the raw edges, adjusting the overlap of the back panels, if necessary. Thoroughly pin and then stitch around all four sides. Finish the seam allowance raw edges by sewing with a zigzag or an overcasting stitch. Trim the corners slightly to reduce bulk and turn the pillow right-side out, gently pushing the corners out as much as possible, using a point turner or other tool such as a knitting needle if necessary. Exercise caution when working the pillow corners into shape so the loosely woven burlap doesn't come apart at the seams. Insert the pillow form through the overlapped edges on the pillow back. 🍃

Visit **BLAIR STOCKER'S** blog, *wise craft*, at blairpeter.typepad.com.

Materials

—¾ yd (68.5 cm) medium-weight fabric in a solid color for body of pillow, such as baby wale corduroy, cotton canvas, or twill (Main)

—½ yd (45.5 cm) or 1 fat quarter quilting-weight cotton fabric in a pattern that inspires you to add jewels (Contrast; *shown:* #7874 Luna by Gail Foundation & Maywood Studios)

—¼ yd (23 cm) muslin (this fabric is for backing and won't be seen)

—Coordinating sewing thread

—Swarovski round sew-on/center hole crystals (*shown:* random mixture of 3 mm, 4 mm, and 5 mm crystals in silver, available at fusionbeads.com)

—Size 11° seed beads, clear (these are needed to secure the crystals)

—Beading thread (*shown:* Coats & Clark Art D35, available at many retailers)

—16" (40.5 cm) square pillow form

—Dinner plate to trace around or 11" (28 cm) circle template

—Removable fabric marker

—Beading or straw needle (must be thin enough to pass through the smallest beads you'll be using)

—Pinking shears (optional)

—Point turner (optional)

Finished Size
16" × 16" (40.5 × 40.5 cm)

---

notes

* All seam allowances are ½" (1.3 cm) unless otherwise indicated.

* For explanations of terms and techniques, see Sewing Basics.

* To sew a crystal onto the fabric, use a beading or straw needle and a double strand of beading thread. Bring the needle up from the back of the fabric, in the center of the bead location. Insert the needle through a crystal from the back and slip the crystal down to the surface of the fabric. Thread the needle through a seed bead, then reinsert the needle back through the hole in the crystal, pulling the thread to the fabric wrong side **(figure 1)**. Grasp the seed bead as you pull, sliding the bead down to sit snugly on top of the crystal. Take a small stitch through the fabric behind the crystal or tie a knot in the thread, before moving on to the next crystal location. With the thread secured between crystal locations, a broken

Bejeweled Pillow
by Blair Stocker

This dazzling pillow gets its sparkle from genuine Swarovski crystals handsewn onto the inset fabric. Make your own pattern with the crystals or follow along a patterned fabric to add sparkle just where you want it.

thread will release only a single crystal and bead.

* Beading and straw needles both have a consistent diameter from point to eye, making them ideal for sewing on beads. Some beading needles are very long, for stringing many beads, but for a sewing project such as this one, a shorter needle is preferable.

* Beading thread is stronger for its size than sewing thread is, so it's the best choice for beading. Choose a color close to the bead color; for example, white thread with silver beads. If beading thread is unavailable, choose a strong polyester sewing thread. Cotton thread is easily shredded by glass bead edges, causing it to break during use.

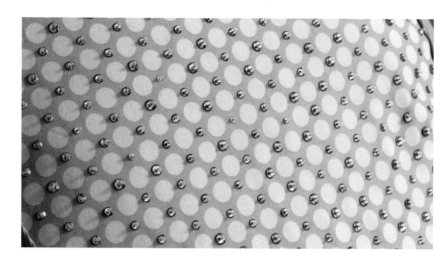

Directions

Cut fabric

1 Cut a 17" × 17" (43 × 43 cm) pillow Front panel and two 17" × 11½" (43 × 29 cm) pillow Back panels from Main fabric.

2 Cut one 17" × 17" (43 × 43 cm) piece of Contrast fabric.

3 Cut one 17" × 17" (43 × 43 cm) piece of muslin.

Create inset on front panel

4 Lay the pillow Front panel, wrong-side up, on your worktable. Fold into quarters and lightly press to find the center of the panel. Position your dinner plate or circle template in the center of this panel, centering it top to bottom and side to side. Trace the plate or circle with a removable fabric marker.

5 Carefully cut out the inside of this circle, leaving a generous ¼" (6 mm) seam allowance inside the line you've drawn. Do not cut on the line. Clip into the seam allowance inside and along the drawn line, cutting up to but not into the line.

6 Layer the panels on your work surface, right sides up, from bottom to top: muslin panel, Contrast fabric panel, and Main fabric Front panel. Smooth and pin these layers together in several places.

7 Edgestitch around the circle's pressed edge, through all layers, stitching on the Main fabric Front panel. These 3 layers will become the pillow front.

8 You're now ready to sew on the crystals. Using a beading or straw needle and coordinating thread, sew the crystals and beads onto the Contrast fabric as desired or follow the pattern on the print fabric (see Notes).

Finish pillow

9 Fold ½" (1.3 cm) to the wrong side of one Back panel, along a 17" (43 cm) edge, and press. Fold an additional ½" (1.3 cm) to the wrong side along the same edge and press again. Repeat with the second Back panel. Zigzag stitch along the inside edge of each hem, covering the folded edge.

10 Bring the 2 Back panels together wrong sides facing up, with the hemmed edges overlapping by 4" (10 cm), to form a 17" (43 cm) square. Pin the overlapping edges. Flip the panels over so that the right side is facing up. Place the assembled pillow front on the Back panels, right sides together. Thoroughly pin and then stitch around all four sides. Finish the seam allowances with pinking shears, by serging, or with a sewing machine zigzag or overcasting stitch. Trim the corners diagonally and turn the pillow right-side out through the overlapped Back panels, gently pushing the corners out as much as possible (use a point turner or similar tool if necessary). Insert the pillow form. 🖋

FIGURE 1

Visit **BLAIR STOCKER'S** blog, *wise craft*, at blairpeter.typepad.com.

Mixed-Media Pillow Cover

by Julie Fei-Fan Balzer

Make use of fabric scraps and unleash your creativity at the same time. Add a personal touch and signature style to this removable patchwork pillow cover with stamping and embellishment.

Materials

—Stamps (Foam and other bold stamps work best.)

—Acrylic paint

—Assorted print fabrics

—14" × 14" (35.5 × 35.5 cm) pillow form

—Paintbrush (optional)

Directions

1 Load a stamp with acrylic paint and stamp on your fabric. This is called overprinting (printing over your already printed fabric). Or you can simply grab a paintbrush and doodle all over your fabric to create a design. This is one of my favorite ways to rescue print fabrics that I don't love and give them new life. Let dry.

Note: Fabrics stamped and painted with acrylic paint will not be machine washable.

2 Cut your stamped fabrics into strips of the same width (or varying sizes, depending on the look you want). For a basic strip design (see the 2 pillows in the middle and back of the photo), cut 2" (5 cm) wide strips. The length of the strips doesn't matter.

3 Sew the strips end to end to make strips that are at least 35" (89 cm) long.

4 Sew the strips together along the long edges to create a large piece of strip-pieced fabric that's at least 16" (40.5 cm) wide.

Variation

Since any fabric with a straight edge can be strip pieced without issue, you can add in orphan blocks from quilts never completed.

5 You will need to cut 3 pieces from the strip-pieced fabric: a 15" × 15" (38 × 38 cm) square for the front, a 15" × 12" (38 × 30.5 cm) rectangle for the back bottom, and a 15" × 6" (38 × 15 cm) rectangle for the back top.

6 Hem the 2 back pieces where they will overlap on the back of the pillow cover (along one 15" [38 cm] edge for each piece).

7 Place the large pillow front square right-side up. Place the hemmed pillow back rectangles (right-side down) on the front square. Align the raw edges (the pillow back pieces will overlap about 3" [7.5 cm]). Be sure the hemmed edges are in the middle. Pin around the perimeter of the pillow cover.

8 Stitch a ¼" (6 mm) seam all around the pinned pillow cover, including where the 2 flaps overlap. Be sure to backstitch at the beginning and end of your stitching.

9 When you've finished stitching, turn the pillow cover right-side out. Use a pen (with the cap on) or another pointy tool to push out the corners. Avoid using anything sharp that might poke through the fabric and make a hole.

10 Slip in the pillow form and place it on your couch! 🍃

Visit **JULIE FEI-FAN BALZER** online at balzerdesigns.typepad.com.

Materials

For two 18" (45.5 cm) pillows

—Choice of 8–12 similar motifs in multiple sizes (Use no more than 6 per pillow.)

—Coordinating fabrics, 2 squares 18½" × 18½" (47 × 47 cm) plus scraps for the pillow front patchwork

—Muslin or paper for layout guide, 18½" × 18½" (47 × 47 cm)

—Lightweight batting

—18" (45.5 cm) pillow forms (2)

notes

∗ Use ½" (1.3 cm) seam allowances throughout.

∗ There is no set number or size of motifs, but to keep the pillow visually balanced, I recommend using no more than 6 per pillow. For these pillows, I used 2 large motifs (cut to approximately 9" × 12" [23 × 30.5 cm]) and various smaller images (cut to about 5" × 7" [12.5 × 18 cm]). I trimmed each piece as necessary to fit within the planned pillow size, allowing for gaps between the motifs to insert some coordinating fabrics.

Directions

1 Cut a piece of muslin or paper 18½" × 18½" (47 × 47 cm) to use as your layout guide. Audition all of your chosen fabrics in different positions on the template until you are pleased with the layout.

2 Using the layout guide, stitch all of your pieces together, and then trim the piece to 18½" × 18½" (47 × 47 cm). Repeat this process for the second pillow top.

3 If you wish, use embroidery floss to handstitch around 2 or 3 of the motifs to help tie the layout together.

4 With right sides together, stitch the pillow front to the back, leaving 1 side open. Trim the corners and turn the pillowcase right-side out.

5 Place the pillow form inside the pillowcase, making sure the corners of the form are correctly placed inside the pillowcase corners and the shape is not warped or pulling.

6 Handstitch the opening closed. Repeat for the second pillow. 🍃

Visit **MARGARET APPLIN** online at margaretapplin.com.

Weeds & Wildflowers
SOFA PILLOW
by Margaret Applin

I turned some photos of weeds and wildflowers into Thermofax screens for printing on fabric. The resulting pillows have a bold graphic look that really "pops" off my sofa. No screen prints? No worries! Use any large-scale commercial fabric or transferred images for this project.

Circles, Stitches & Dye
by Jill Brummett Tucker

I like to combine dissimilar patterns and colors, which makes dressing in suitable outfits challenging, but serves me well in fiber arts. I also enjoy dyeing fabric and free-motion stitching. When I read an article in *Quilting Arts* by Malka Dubrawsky in which she explained a Japanese dye process called *itajime*, I was inspired to figure out how I could combine dyeing, free-motion stitching, and *itajime* into one piece of artwork.

Materials
For one pillow

—Assorted fabrics, 9 squares 6" × 6" (15 × 15 cm)

—Coordinating fabric for backing, 2 pieces 11" × 17" (28 × 43 cm)

—Thread

—Embroidery thread

—Tear-away fabric stabilizer

—Buttons (2)

—Pillow form, 16" × 16" (40.5 × 40.5 cm)

—2 identical Plexiglas shapes, such as (2) 4" (10 cm) diameter circles and (2) 6½" (16.5 cm) squares with a circle cut out of the middle of each (Check for Plexiglas at your local hardware store. You may be able to have them cut it to size.)

—C-clamps (4)

—Calibrated bucket

—Shallow plastic dishpans (3)

—Rubber gloves

—Eye protection

—Respirator (Use a cartridge respirator fitted with an acid gas cartridge.)

—Liquid Rit dye in various colors

—Bleach

—Anti-Chlor Concentrate

Directions
Dyeing fabric blocks
You can dye all of your fabric blocks or you can discharge some of them. I chose to do a little of both for my pillows, but your finished pillow will look great whatever you decide.

1 Position 2 of the 6" × 6" (15 × 15 cm) fabric squares between 2 of your matching Plexiglas shapes. Place the Plexiglas over where you would like the design to be and secure with the 4 C-clamps.

2 Using the calibrated bucket, measure and pour 2 quarts of hot water into your dishpan.

Note: The water must be deep enough so that the fabric will be completely submerged when you put it in the dye bath, so adjust accordingly.

3 Pour in the dye. The amount of dye you use depends on the effect you

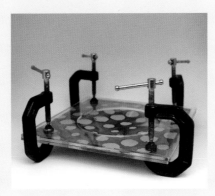

The *itajime* process involves clamping fabric between two identical Plexiglas shapes and then dyeing (or discharging the fabric to remove color), thus protecting the covered area of the fabric from the dye (or discharge) and leaving a design. Adding my personal spin to the *itajime* process, I dyed and discharged random fabric blocks and then embellished them with fresh, fun stitches to create lively pillows. The best part about this process is that you can never accurately predict how each dyed-and-stitched block will turn out. The element of mystery enhances the experience.

seek. The more dye you add, the more intense the color will be.

4 Wearing rubber gloves, submerge your clamped fabric and then let it sit for 10–60 minutes, depending how deep you want the dye color.

5 When you have the color you want, remove the clamped fabric and pour the dye bath down the kitchen drain. Rinse your fabric (still in the clamped Plexiglas sandwich).

6 Disassemble the sandwich, rinse your fabric again, and wash it.

Tip

You can repeat the dye process with different colors of dye on different fabric blocks, or dye them all the same color. It is also possible to mix different dye colors together.

7 Dry and press all of your dyed blocks.

Discharging fabric blocks

Caution: Follow the manufacturer's safety instructions when using Anti-Chlor, including wearing safety glasses, rubber gloves, and a cartridge respirator fitted with an acid gas cartridge. Work outside in a well-ventilated location.

8 Position 2 of your 6" × 6" (15 × 15 cm) fabric squares between 2 matching Plexiglas shapes and secure with 4 C-clamps.

9 Place 2 dishpans right next to each other on a sturdy outdoor surface.

10 Using the calibrated bucket, measure and pour 2 quarts of hot water and 1 cup of bleach into the first dishpan.

11 Into the other dishpan pour 2 quarts of warm water and ¼ teaspoon of Anti-Chlor.

Note: The water in both dishpans must be deep enough so that the fabric will be completely submerged, so adjust accordingly.

12 Wearing your rubber gloves, eye protection, and respirator, submerge the clamped fabric in the bleach bath. Swish it gently and watch for the color to fade.

13 When the color has faded as much as you want, rinse the clamped fabric with cold water to remove as much bleach as possible.

14 Disassemble the fabric and Plexiglas, and then quickly submerge the fabric into the Anti-Chlor; keep it in the bath for 5 minutes. (This stops the bleach from removing more color.)

15 Remove and rinse the fabric again with cold water.

16 Wash the fabric in a small amount of laundry detergent and cold water.

17 Pour the bleach water down the drain, and then let the water run down the drain for 20 seconds. Pour the Anti-Chlor water down a different drain.

18 Dry and press your discharged blocks.

Creating a pillow with an envelope back

Note: All seams are ¼" (6 mm) unless otherwise noted. Before you begin to sew anything, lay the blocks on your table and try different placements until you get the arrangement just right.

19 With regular thread, stitch the blocks together in 3 rows of 3, and then stitch the rows together. Press the pillow front.

20 Secure the fabric stabilizer to the corners of each of the 9 blocks that you have just stitched together.

21 Stitch the front of each block with embroidery thread using a free-motion foot. Tear away the fabric stabilizer. (Some of the stabilizer will stay put due to the free-motion stitching and that's okay.)

22 For each pillow back piece, turn a hem along 1 long side and press. Turn another hem and press again, and then stitch the hems.

23 Sew 2 buttonholes onto 1 side of the pillow back 1½" (3.8 cm) from the hem seam.

24 Place the pillow back panel with the buttonholes onto the pillow front (right sides together). Align the raw edges and pin.

25 Align the second pillow back panel on the pillow front and pin. The 2 sections of the pillow back should now be overlapping with the buttonhole piece being closest to the pillow front.

26 Stitch with regular thread around all edges and then trim the corners and any excess fabric.

27 Turn the pillow right-side out and sew the 2 buttons in place, aligning them with the placement of the buttonholes.

28 Gently insert your pillow form, close the buttons, and toss your new pillow in that perfect place.

Note: Rit dyes will fade with repeated washing, so I recommend spot cleaning only. 🍃

Visit **JILL BRUMMETT TUCKER'S** website at jbtucker.net.

Holiday Ornament PILLOW
by Debbie Grifka

Pillow covers are such a fast and fun way to perk up your décor, especially for the holidays. One of the great features of this pillow design is its versatility. It works well in red and white, or in an elegant cream tone with dark ornaments, or with ornaments of different colors or patterns. The simple shape also makes a perfect canvas for fussy cutting or embellishment, and it's easy to adapt this design to match your own décor.

Materials

—Removable marking pencil or chalk

—Ornament template on page 50

—Red fabric for front, 17" × 17" (43 × 43 cm) square

—Red fabric for back, 2 squares 13" × 17" (33 × 43 cm) each

—White tone-on-tone scraps, 7 pieces each 2½" × 6" (6.5 × 15 cm)

—Fusible web, 1 piece 5" × 20" (12.5 × 51 cm)

—Batting, 17" × 17" (43 × 43 cm) square

—Muslin or other lining fabric, 17" × 17" (43 × 43 cm) square

—Pillow form, 16" × 16" (40.5 × 40.5 cm) square

Directions

1 Trace the ornament template onto the fusible web 7 times, leaving ½" (1.3 cm) between shapes. Cut out the ornament shapes, cutting approximately ¼" (6 mm) outside the traced lines.

2 Following the fusible instructions, adhere the ornament shapes to the back of the white tone-on-tone fabrics. Cut out the ornaments along the traced lines and set aside.

3 Mark the ornament placement lines on the red 17" × 17" (43 × 43 cm) pillow front fabric as follows: Using a removable marking pencil (or chalk), draw a line from the top pillow edge to the bottom edge 4" (10 cm) from the right raw edge of the pillow front. Draw a second line 6" (15 cm) from the right raw edge of the pillow front. Make a mark 2½" (6.5 cm) from the bottom edge along the second line.**(figure 1)**.

4 Center the first ornament on the first line, with the ornament tip touching the bottom raw edge of the pillow front. Leaving ½" (1.3 cm) between ornaments, center 2 additional ornaments along the first line **(Figure 2)**.

5 For the second line of ornaments, start by placing the first full ornament so that its tip is at the 2½" (6.5 cm) mark. Leaving ½" (1.3 cm) between ornaments, position 2 additional ornaments above this one, centering them on the line (the top ornament will extend beyond the raw edge). Place the final ornament ½" (1.3 cm) below the bottom ornament. Trim the ornaments that fall beyond the raw edge of the pillow front.

6 Fuse the ornaments in place, and satin-stitch the raw edges.

7 To mark the remaining red area on the pillow front for quilting, draw lines every 2" (5 cm; parallel to the ones with the fused ornaments) and trace the ornament shapes, positioning them in the same manner as above.

8 Layer the pillow front with the batting and muslin lining. Quilt the pillow front.

9 To make the pillow back, turn under a long raw edge on each of the 13" × 17" (33 × 43 cm) pieces twice, press and topstitch in place.

10 Place the quilted pillow front right-side up and layer the pillow back pieces on top, with the right sides facing the pillow front and all raw edges aligned. The topstitched edges should overlap each other in the middle of the pillow back. Stitch a ½" (1.3 cm) seam around all 4 sides of the pillow cover.

11 Trim the corners. Turn the cover right-side out and press. Insert the pillow form and enjoy. 🖉

Visit **DEBBIE GRIFKA** online at eschhousequilts.blogspot.com.

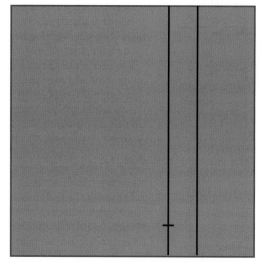

FIGURE 1

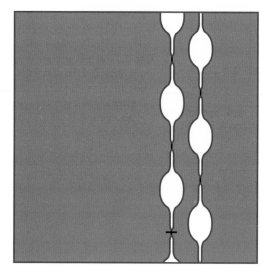

FIGURE 2

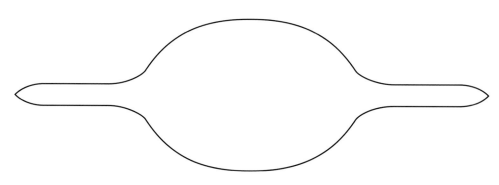

Ornament template
(actual size)

Sewing Basics
A quick reference guide to basic tools, techniques, and terms

For the projects in this issue (unless otherwise indicated):

* When piecing: Use ¼" (6 mm) seam allowances. Stitch with the right sides together. After stitching a seam, press it to set the seam; then open the fabrics and press the seam allowance toward the darker fabric.

* Yardages are based upon 44" (112 cm) wide fabric.

Sewing Kit

The following items are essential for your sewing kit. Make sure you have these tools on hand before starting any of the projects:

* **ACRYLIC RULER** This is a clear flat ruler, with a measuring grid at least 2" × 18" (5 × 45.5 cm). A rigid acrylic (quilter's) ruler should be used when working with a rotary cutter. You should have a variety of rulers in different shapes and sizes.

* **BATTING** 100% cotton, 100% wool, plus bamboo, silk, and blends.

* **BONE FOLDER** Allows you to make non-permanent creases in fabric, paper, and other materials.

* **CRAFT SCISSORS** To use when cutting out paper patterns.

* **EMBROIDERY SCISSORS** These small scissors are used to trim off threads, clip corners, and do other intricate cutting work.

* **FABRIC** Commercial prints, hand-dyes, cottons, upholstery, silks, wools; the greater the variety of types, colors, designs, and textures, the better.

* **FABRIC MARKING PENS/PENCILS + TAILOR'S CHALK** Available in several colors for use on light and dark fabrics; use to trace patterns and pattern markings onto your fabric. Tailor's chalk is available in triangular pieces, rollers, and pencils. Some forms (such as powdered) can simply be brushed away; refer to the manufacturer's instructions for the recommended removal method for your chosen marking tool.

* **FREE-MOTION OR DARNING FOOT** Used to free-motion quilt.

* **FUSIBLE WEB** Used to fuse fabrics together. There are a variety of products on the market.

* **GLUE** Glue stick, fabric glue, and all-purpose glue.

* **HANDSEWING + EMBROIDERY NEEDLES** Keep an assortment of sewing and embroidery needles in different sizes, from fine to sturdy.

* **IRON, IRONING BOARD + PRESS CLOTHS** An iron is an essential tool when sewing. Use cotton muslin or silk organza as a press cloth to protect delicate fabric surfaces from direct heat. Use a Teflon sheet or parchment paper to protect your iron and ironing board when working with fusible web.

* **MEASURING TAPE** Make sure it's at least 60" (152.5 cm) long and retractable.

* **NEEDLE THREADER** An inexpensive aid to make threading the eye of the needle super fast.

* **PINKING SHEARS** These scissors with notched teeth leave a zigzag edge on the cut cloth to prevent fraying.

* **POINT TURNER** A blunt, pointed tool that helps push out the corners of a project and/or smooth seams. A knitting needle or chopstick may also be used.

* **ROTARY CUTTER + SELF-HEALING MAT** Useful for cutting out fabric quickly. Always use a mat to protect the blade and your work surface (a rigid acrylic ruler should be used with a rotary cutter to make straight cuts).

* **SAFTEY PINS** Always have a bunch on hand.

* **SCISSORS** Heavy-duty shears reserved for fabric only; a pair of small, sharp embroidery scissors; thread snips; a pair of all-purpose scissors; pinking shears.

* **SEAM RIPPER** Handy for quickly ripping out stitches.

* **SEWING MACHINE** With free-motion capabilities.

* **STRAIGHT PINS + PINCUSHION** Always keep lots of pins nearby.

* **TEMPLATE SUPPLIES** Keep freezer paper or other large paper (such as parchment paper) on hand for tracing the templates you intend to use. Regular office paper may be used for templates that will fit. You should also have card stock or plastic if you wish to make permanent templates that can be reused.

* **THIMBLE** Your fingers and thumbs will thank you.

* **THREAD** All types, including hand and machine thread for stitching and quilting; variegated; metallic; 100% cotton; monofilament.

* **ZIPPER FOOT** An accessory foot for your machine with a narrow profile that can be positioned to sew close to the zipper teeth. A zipper foot is adjustable so the foot can be moved to either side of the needle.

Glossary of Sewing Terms and Techniques

BACKSTITCH Stitching in reverse for a short distance at the beginning and end of a seam line to secure the stitches. Most machines have a button or knob for this function (also called backtack).

BASTING Using long, loose stitches to hold something in place temporarily. To baste by machine, use the longest straight stitch length available on your machine. To baste by hand, use stitches at least ¼" (6 mm) long. Use a contrasting thread to make the stitches easier to spot for removal.

BIAS The direction across a fabric that is located at a 45-degree angle from the lengthwise or crosswise grain. The bias has high stretch and a very fluid drape.

BIAS TAPE Made from fabric strips cut on a 45-degree angle to the grainline, the bias cut creates an edging fabric that will stretch to enclose smooth or curved edges. You can buy bias tape ready-made or make your own.

CLIPPING CURVES Involves cutting tiny slits or triangles into the seam allowance of curved edges so the seam will lie flat when turned right-side out. Cut slits along concave curves and triangles (with points toward the seam line) along a convex curve. Be careful not to clip into the stitches.

CLIP THE CORNERS Clipping the corners of a project reduces bulk and allows for crisper corners in the finished project. To clip a corner, cut off a triangle-shaped piece of fabric across the seam allowances at the corner. Cut close to the seam line but be careful not to cut through the stitches.

DART This stitched triangular fold is used to give shape and form to the fabric to fit body curves.

EDGESTITCH A row of topstitching placed very close (1/16"–1/8" [2–3 mm]) to an edge or an existing seam line.

FABRIC GRAIN The grain is created in a woven fabric by the threads that travel lengthwise and crosswise. The lengthwise grain runs parallel to the selvedges; the crosswise grain should always be perpendicular to the lengthwise threads. If the grains aren't completely straight and perpendicular, grasp the fabric at diagonally opposite corners and pull gently to restore the grain. In knit fabrics, the lengthwise grain runs along the wales (ribs), parallel to the selvedges, with the crosswise grain running along the courses (perpendicular to the wales).

FINGER-PRESS Pressing a fold or crease with your fingers as opposed to using an iron.

FUSSY-CUT Cutting a specific motif from a commercial or hand-printed fabric. Generally used to center a motif in a patchwork pattern or to feature a specific motif in an appliqué design. Use a clear acrylic ruler or template plastic to isolate the selected motif and ensure that it will fit within the desired size, including seam allowances.

GRAINLINE A pattern marking showing the direction of the grain. Make sure the grainline marked on the pattern runs parallel to the lengthwise grain of your fabric, unless the grainline is specifically marked as crosswise or bias.

INTERFACING Material used to stabilize or reinforce fabrics. Fusible interfacing has an adhesive coating on one side that adheres to fabric when ironed.

LINING The inner fabric of a garment or bag, used to create a finished interior that covers the raw edges of the seams.

MITER Joining a seam or fold at an angle that bisects the project corner. Most common is a 45-degree angle, like a picture frame, but shapes other than squares or rectangles will have miters with different angles.

OVERCAST STITCH A machine stitch that wraps around the fabric raw edge to finish edges and prevent unraveling. Some sewing machines have several overcast stitch options; consult your sewing machine manual for information on stitch settings and the appropriate presser foot for the chosen stitch (often the standard presser foot can be used). A zigzag stitch can be used as an alternative to finish raw edges if your machine doesn't have an overcast stitch function.

PRESHRINK Many fabrics shrink when washed; you need to wash, dry, and press all your fabric before you start to sew, following the suggested cleaning method marked on the fabric bolt (keep in mind that the appropriate cleaning method may not be machine washing). Don't skip this step!

RIGHT SIDE The front side, or the side that should be on the outside of a finished garment. On a print fabric, the print will be stronger on the right side of the fabric.

RIGHT SIDES TOGETHER The right sides of two fabric layers should be facing each other.

SATIN STITCH (MACHINE) This is a smooth, completely filled column of zigzag stitches achieved by setting the stitch length short enough for complete coverage but long enough to prevent bunching and thread buildup.

SEAM ALLOWANCE The amount of fabric between the raw edge and the seam.

SELVEDGE This is the tightly woven border on the lengthwise edges of woven fabric and the finished lengthwise edges of knit fabric.

SQUARING UP After you have pieced together a fabric block or section, check to make sure the edges are straight and the measurements are correct. Use a rotary cutter and an acrylic ruler to trim the block if necessary.

STITCH IN THE DITCH Lay the quilt sandwich right-side up under the presser foot and sew along the seam line "ditch." The stitches will fall between the two fabric pieces and disappear into the seam.

TOPSTITCH Used to hold pieces firmly in place and/or to add a decorative effect, a topstitch is simply a stitch that can be seen on the outside of the garment or piece. To topstitch, make a line of stitching on the outside (right side) of the piece, usually a set distance from an existing seam.

UNDERSTITCHING A line of stitches placed on a facing (or lining), very near the facing/garment seam. Understitching is used to hold the seam allowances and facing together and to prevent the facing from rolling toward the outside of the garment.

WRONG SIDE The wrong side of the fabric is the underside, or the side that should be on the inside of a finished garment. On a print fabric, the print will be lighter or less obvious on the wrong side of the fabric.

Stitch Glossary

Backstitch
Working from right to left, bring the needle up at **1** and insert behind the starting point at **2**. Bring the needle up at **3**, repeat by inserting at **1** and bringing the needle up at a point that is a stitch length beyond **3**.

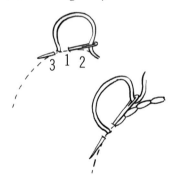

Basting Stitch
Using the longest straight stitch length on your machine, baste to temporarily hold fabric layers and seams in position for final stitching. It can also be done by hand. When basting, use a contrasting thread to make it easier to spot when you're taking it out.

Blanket Stitch
Working from left to right, bring the needle up at **1** and insert at **2**. Bring the needle back up at **3** and over the working thread. Repeat by making the next stitch in the same manner, keeping the spacing even.

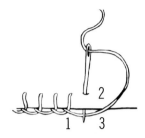

Blindstitch/Blind-Hem Stitch
Used mainly for hemming fabrics where an inconspicuous hem is difficult to achieve (this stitch is also useful for securing binding on the wrong side). Fold the hem edge back about ¼" (6 mm). Take a small stitch in the garment, picking up only a few threads of the fabric, then take the next stitch ¼" (6 mm) ahead in the hem. Continue, alternating stitches between the hem and the garment (if using for a non-hemming application, simply alternate stitches between the two fabric edges being joined).

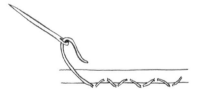

Chain Stitch
Working from top to bottom, bring the needle up at and reinsert at **1** to create a loop; do not pull the thread taut. Bring the needle back up at **2**, keeping the needle above the loop and gently pulling the needle toward you to tighten the loop flush to the fabric.

Repeat by inserting the needle at **2** to form a loop and bring the needle up at **3**. Tack the last loop down with a straight stitch.

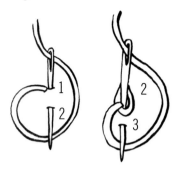

Straight Stitch + Running Stitch
Working from right to left, make a straight stitch by bringing the needle up and insert at **1**, ⅛"–¼" (3–6 mm) from the starting point. To make a line of running stitches (a row of straight stitches worked one after the other), bring the needle up at **2** and repeat.

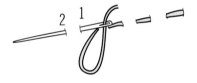

French Knot
Bring the needle up at **1** and hold the thread taut above the fabric. Point the needle toward your fingers and move the needle in a circular motion to wrap the thread around the needle once or twice. Insert the needle near **1** and hold the thread taut near the knot as you pull the needle and thread through the knot and the fabric to complete.

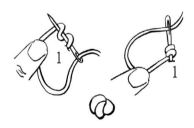

Couching

Working from right to left, use one thread, known as the couching or working thread, to tack down one or more strands of fiber, known as the couched fibers. Bring the working thread up at **1** and insert at **2**, over the fibers to tack them down, bringing the needle back up at **3**. The fibers are now encircled by the couching thread. Repeat to couch the desired length of fiber(s). This stitch may also be worked from left to right, and the spacing between the couching threads may vary for different design effects.

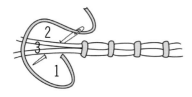

Cross-Stitch

Working from right to left, bring the needle up at **1**, insert at **2**, then bring the needle back up at **3**. Finish by inserting the needle at **4**. Repeat for the desired number of stitches.

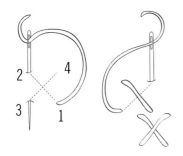

Whipstitch

Bring the needle up at **1**, insert at **2**, and bring up at **3**. These quick stitches do not have to be very tight or close together.

Standard Hand-Appliqué Stitch

Cut a length of thread 12"–18" (30.5–45.5 cm). Thread the newly cut end through the eye of the needle, pull this end through, and knot it. Use this technique to thread the needle and knot the thread to help keep the thread's "twist" intact and to reduce knotting. Beginning at the straightest edge of the appliqué and working from right to left, bring the needle up from the underside, through the background fabric and the very edge of the appliqué at **1**, catching only a few threads of the appliqué fabric. Pull the thread taut, then insert the needle into the background fabric at **2**, as close as possible to **1**. Bring the needle up through the background fabric at **3**, ⅛" (3 mm) beyond **2**. Continue in this manner, keeping the thread taut (do not pull it so tight that the fabric puckers) to keep the stitching as invisible as possible.

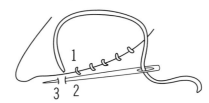

Slip Stitch

Working from right to left, join two pieces of fabric by taking a ¹⁄₁₆"–¼" (2–6 mm) long stitch into the folded edge of one piece of fabric and bringing the needle out. Insert the needle into the folded edge of the other piece of fabric, directly across from the point where the thread emerged from the previous stitch. Repeat by inserting the needle into the first piece of fabric. The thread will be almost entirely hidden inside the folds of the fabrics.

Create Binding

Cutting Straight Strips

Cut strips on the crosswise grain, from selvedge to selvedge. Use a rotary cutter and straightedge to obtain a straight cut. Remove the selvedges and join the strips with diagonal seams (see instructions at right).

Cutting Bias Strips

Fold one cut end of the fabric to meet one selvedge, forming a fold at a 45-degree angle to the selvedge (**1**). With the fabric placed on a self-healing mat, cut off the fold with a rotary cutter, using a straightedge as a guide to make a straight cut. With the straightedge and rotary cutter, cut strips to the appropriate width (**2**). Join the strips with diagonal seams.

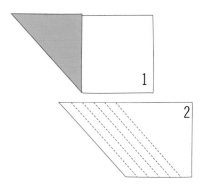

Binding with Mitered Corners

Decide whether you will use a Double-fold Binding (option A at right) or a Double-layer Binding (option B at right). *If using double-layer binding follow the alternate italicized instructions in parenthesis.*

Open the binding and press ½" (1.3 cm) to the wrong side at one short end (*refold the binding at the center crease and proceed*). Starting with the folded-under end of the binding, place it near the center of the first edge of the project to be bound, matching the raw edges, and pin in place. Begin sewing near the center of one edge of the project, along the first crease (*at the appropriate distance from the raw edge*), leaving several inches of the binding fabric free at the beginning. Stop sewing ¼" (6 mm) before reaching the corner, backstitch, and cut the threads. Rotate the project 90 degrees to position it for sewing the next side. Fold the binding fabric up, away from the project, at a 45-degree angle (**1**), then fold it back down along the project raw edge (**2**). This forms a miter at the corner. Stitch the second side, beginning at the project raw edge (**2**) and ending ¼" (6 mm) from the next corner, as before.

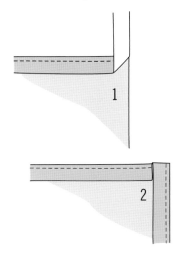

Continue as established until you have completed the last corner. Continue stitching until you are a few inches from the beginning edge of the binding fabric. Overlap the pressed beginning edge of the binding by ½" (1.3 cm) (or overlap more as necessary for security) and trim the working edge to fit. Finish sewing the binding *(opening the center fold and tucking the raw edge inside the pressed end of the binding strip)*. Refold the binding along all the creases and then fold it over the project raw edges to the back, enclosing the raw edges *(there are no creases to worry about with option B)*. The folded edge of the binding strip should just cover the stitches visible on the project back. Slip-stitch or blindstitch the binding in place, tucking in the corners to complete the miters as you go (**3**).

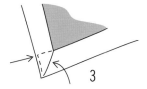

Diagonal Seams for Joining Strips

Lay two strips right sides together, at right angles. The area where the strips overlap forms a square. Sew diagonally across the square as shown above. Trim the excess fabric ¼" (6 mm) away from the seam line and press the seam allowances open. Repeat to join all the strips, forming one long fabric band.

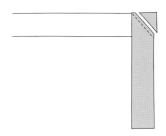

Fold Binding

A. Double-fold Binding

This option will create binding that is similar to packaged double-fold bias tape/binding. Fold the strip in half lengthwise, with wrong sides together; press. Open up the fold and then fold each long edge toward the wrong side, so that the raw edges meet in the middle (**1**). Refold the binding along the existing center crease, enclosing the raw edges (**2**), and press again.

B. Double-layer Binding

This option creates a double-thick binding with only one fold. This binding is often favored by quilters. Fold the strip in half lengthwise with wrong sides together; press.

Find popular patterns for quick and easy projects with these *Craft Tree* publications, brought to you by Interweave.

Evening Bags
ISBN 978-1-59668-764-6

Everyday Totes
ISBN 978-1-59668-774-5

Fun Home Accessories
ISBN 978-1-59668-769-1

Just for Baby
ISBN 978-1-59668-773-8

Just for Kids
ISBN 978-1-59668-772-1

Modern Sewing Projects
ISBN 978-1-59668-768-4

Notebook Covers
ISBN 978-1-59668-766-0

Patchwork Pillows
ISBN 978-1-59668-767-7

Scarves and Wraps
ISBN 978-1-59668-770-7

Teacher Gifts
ISBN 978-1-59668-765-3

Travel Accessories
ISBN 978-1-59668-771-4

Visit your favorite retailer or order online at interweavestore.com

INTERWEAVE.
interweavestore.com